OAKWOOD LIBRARY OF RAILWAY HIS

The
BIDEFORD, WESTWARD HO! & APPLEDORE RAILWAY

by
Stanley C. Jenkins, MA

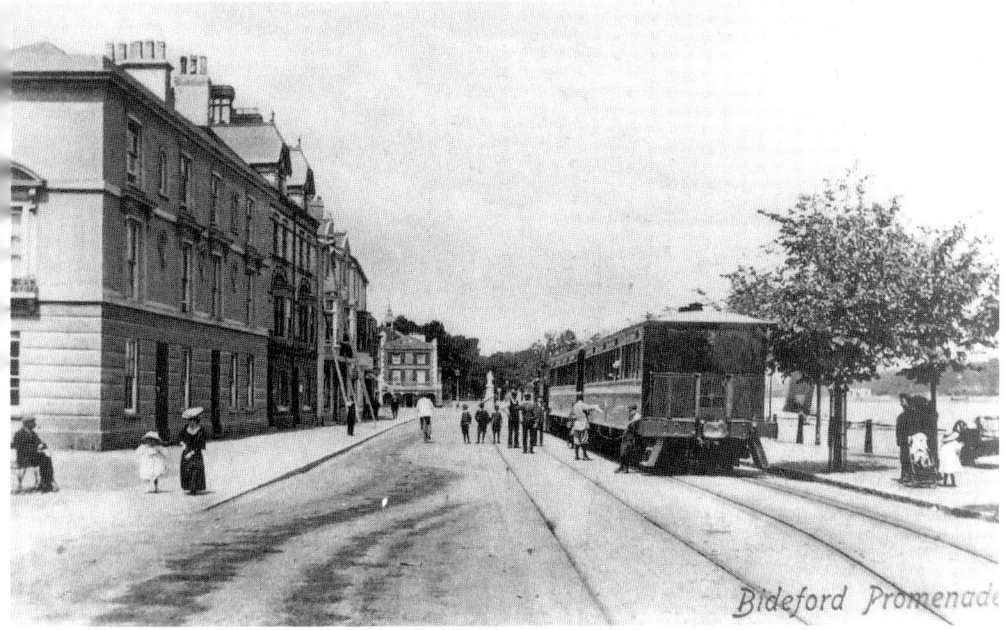

THE OAKWOOD PRESS

© S.C. Jenkins and Oakwood Press 1993

ISBN 0 85361 452 0

Typeset by Gem Publishing Company, Brightwell, Wallingford, Oxfordshire.
Printed by Cambrian Printers, Aberystwyth

All rights reserved. No part of this book may be reproduced or transmitted in any form or by any means, electronic or mechanical, including photo-copying, recording or by any information storage and retrieval system, without permission from the Publisher in writing.

Title page. A two-coach train pauses on Bideford Quay during the early 1900s.
Lens of Sutton

BWH&AR locomotive *Torridge* departs from Bideford Quay with a single-coach train. The quay siding diverges in the foreground. *Lens of Sutton*

Published by
The OAKWOOD PRESS
P.O.Box 122, Headington, Oxford.

Contents

	Introduction	7
	Historical Summary	9
Chapter One	**Origins of the Bideford, Westward Ho! & Appledore Railway** Bideford & Appledore — Origins of the Victorian Tourist Industry — The Influence of Charles Kingsley — The Creation of Westward Ho! — Early Railway Schemes — The Bideford, Appledore & Westward Ho! Railway — Light Railway Schemes — The Formation of the Bideford, Westward Ho! & Appledore Railway	11
Chapter Two	**Opening and Early Years of the Westward Ho! Line** Some Details of the 1896 Act of Parliament — The Bideford & Clovelly Railway — Narrow or Standard Gauge? — Disagreement with the Borough Council — Details of the Bideford & Clovelly Act — Construction Begins — The British Electric Traction Takeover — The Scheme Proceeds — Opening of the Line — The Board of Trade Inspection Report — Some Further Details of the Line	27
Chapter Three	**Extension to Appledore** Abandonment of the Clovelly Scheme — Renewed Problems at Bideford — The Light Railway Order of 1904 — Colonel Yorke's Re-inspection — Final Inspection of the Bideford Loop Line — Completion of the Scheme — Opening to Appledore — Boardroom Changes	47
Chapter Four	**The Railway in Operation** Stations and Halts — Train Services — The Locomotives — Passenger Rolling Stock — BWH&AR Goods Rolling Stock — Signalling Notes — Tickets and Fare Collection — BWH&AR Uniforms	61
Chapter Five	**The Route from Bideford to Appledore** Bideford Quay — Bideford Yard — Causeway Crossing Halt — Kenwith Castle Halt — Abbotsham Road — Cornborough Cliffs — Westward Ho! — Northam — Appledore	85
Chapter Six	**Subsequent History and Minor Details** Two Contrasting Glimpses — A Failed Resort? — Proposed Petrol Railcar Operation — Boardroom Changes — World War I — Closure and Requisition — Lost at Sea? — Post-Closure Developments — Further Notes on Trackwork — Staff and Staff Numbers — Bideford, Westward Ho! & Appledore Uniforms — The Railway Today	119
	Sources and Acknowledgments	139
	Appendices	140
	Bibliography	142
	Index	144

Bideford Bridge, looking west towards Bideford. *Oakwood Collection*

A similar view, looking east towards East-the-Water and the LSWR station.
Oakwood Collection

A Note on Nomenclature

To prevent confusion it would be useful to define certain contentious or ambiguous terms at the very outset. The following definitions are used throughout.

TRAMWAY – A localised industrial or freight-only railway, typically worked by horses rather than locomotives.

STREET TRAMWAY – A specialised, mainly passenger-carrying railway laid in a public highway, and worked by horse, steam, internal combustion, cable or electrical power.

RAILWAY – A railway built under the Powers of an Act of Parliament or Light Railway Order, and running on its own right of way.

LIGHT RAILWAY – A cheaply constructed railway, constructed or worked under the terms of the Regulation of Railways Act 1868, the Light Railways Act 1896, or the Light Railways Act 1912 (or, if built in Ireland, under the Light Railways Act of 1889).

LIGHT RAILWAY ORDER – An Order in Council obtained under the Light Railways Acts, enabling railway promoters to construct lines without a specific Act of Parliament.

FENDER – A lightweight structure attached to the front or rear of a railway engine or tramcar to prevent horses or pedestrians from falling under the wheels (i.e. a cow-catcher).

Confusingly, the Bideford, Westward Ho! & Appledore Railway was originally constructed as a *railway* under an Act of Parliament, although it also incorporated a *street tramway* and a section of line built as a *light railway* under the terms of a Light Railway Order. The entire line was, retrospectively, designated a *light railway* under the provisions of the Regulation of Railways Act 1868. However, as the Bideford, Westward Ho! & Appledore Railway (BWH&AR) had been incorporated under the Bideford, Westward Ho! & Appledore Railway Act of 1896, the BWH&AR line was not normally regarded as a light railway and that somewhat ambiguous term was never used as part of the railway's title.

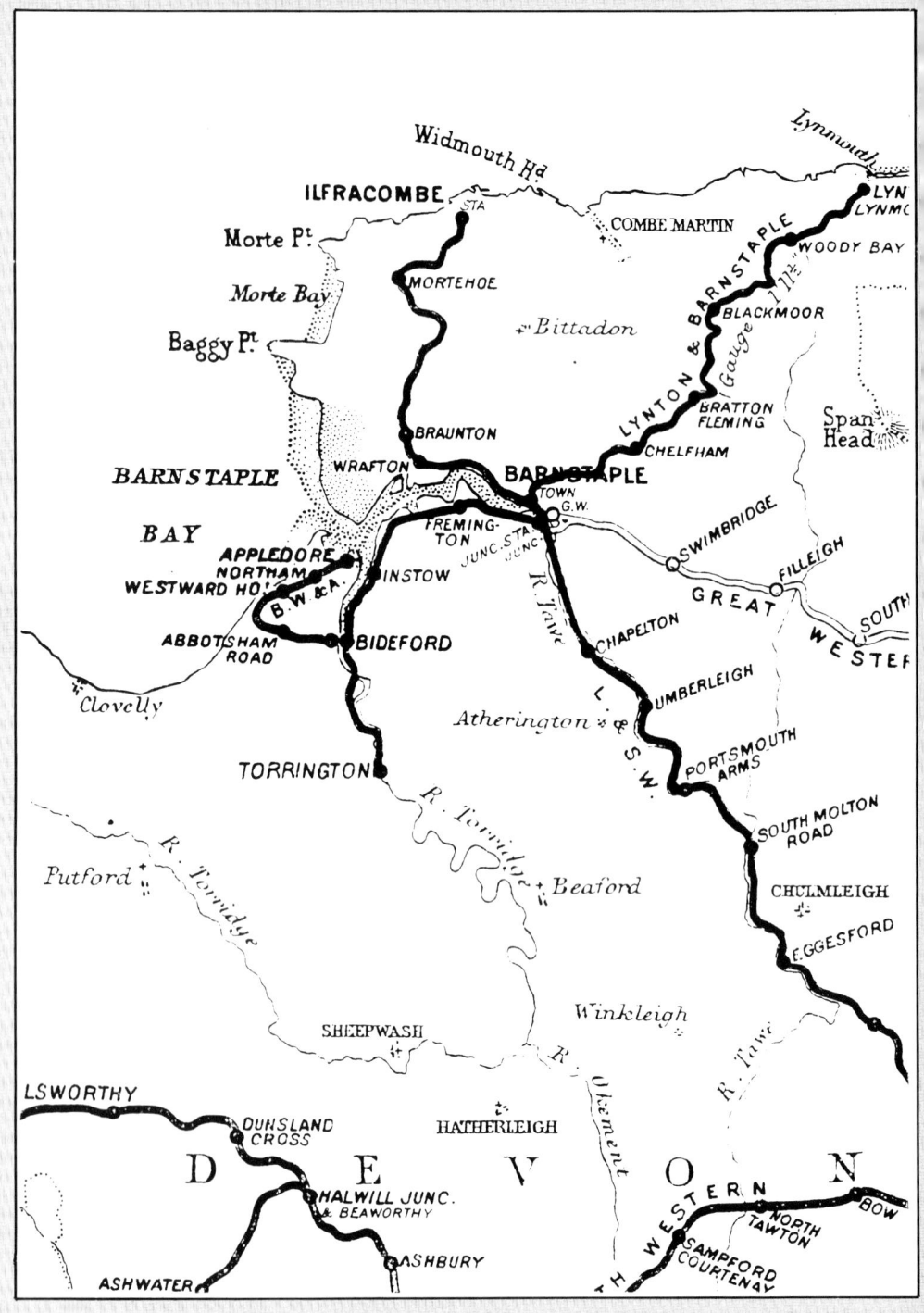

The RCH map of the area.

Introduction

The Bideford, Westward Ho! & Appledore Railway was an isolated single track railway in North Devon. Apart from the fact that it was the only railway in the country to have an exclamation mark in its title, the Westward Ho! line had few claims to fame. This was, at least in part, because the railway had an extraordinarily short life – having opened in 1901 and closed just 16 years later. For this reason, the route never enjoyed the attention of enthusiasts or photographers, and whereas the neighbouring Lynton & Barnstaple Railway became a mecca for minor railway fans during the 1930s, by then the Bideford, Westward Ho! & Appledore Railway had already lapsed into more or less total obscurity.

Another reason why the Westward Ho! line had been neglected concerns its somewhat uncertain status; although obviously a railway line, part of its seven mile route was laid as a street tramway, and the BWH&AR was, moreover, owned by a tramway company rather than a railway. If the route had passed into London & South Western control during the early 1900s it would doubtless have been perceived as a 'proper' railway, and with more aggressive marketing the route might have carried more traffic (and thereby escaped the ignominy of early closure).

Having made these points, it should be said that the Bideford, Westward Ho! & Appledore Railway line exhibited many interesting and attractive features. It was, for example, a scenic route that served a picturesque West Country holiday area, while its small stations, with their compact track layouts, will have obvious appeal for railway modellers.

In historical terms the Westward Ho! line presents several problems of interpretation. It was opened at a time when railways were an accepted part of the national scene, and with large numbers of light railways and tramways being constructed throughout the country, the opening of this North Devon line had little 'news' value for journals such as *The Railway Times* or *The Railway Engineer*. There was, in consequence, very little press coverage of the line – although both of these specialist publications referred to the BWH&AR line on occasions. Local newspapers such as *The Bideford Gazette* contain rather more information for modern researchers, while the Board of Trade records at the Public Record Office provide an unexpectedly good source of technical data for the Westward Ho! line.

There is fortunately, a body of material on the BWH&AR line in record repositories such as the Public Record Office and the University of Leicester library, and it is therefore possible for the history of this obscure railway to be pieced together with the aid of original sources. In fact, the resulting story is surprisingly complex, and although there are inevitably one or two gaps in our knowledge, it is hoped that the following history of the Bideford, Westward Ho! & Appledore Railway will be of interest to railway enthusiasts and railway modellers, as well as local historians and all who have an affection for the West Country and its long and fascinating story.

Stanley C. Jenkins
Witney, Oxfordshire 1993

A panoramic view of Bideford, looking west from a vantage point above the LSWR station. The Bideford, Westward Ho! & Appledore line was situated on the far side of the river – the terminus being just out of site at the top right hand side of the photograph.

Historical Summary

Company of Origin	Bideford, Westward Ho! & Appledore Railway, incorporated by Act of Parliament dated 21st May, 1896, to build a railway from Bideford Quay to Appledore.
Dates of Opening	Bideford to Northam 20th May, 1901. Northam to Appledore (under Light Railway Order) 1st May, 1908.
Length of Line	7 miles 4 chains.
Mode of Operation of single line	Train-staff-and-ticket in conjunction with ordinary telephone; intermediate crossing loops at Abbotsham Road, Westward Ho! and Bideford Yard.
Steepest gradient	1 in 40 (between Abbotsham Road and Westward Ho!).
Locomotives	Three Hunslet-built 2–4–2Ts (Works Nos. 713/714/715).
Rolling Stock	Six bogie passenger vehicles, one brake van and eight goods vehicles.
Directors (1903)	Captain George Frederick Molesworth RN, F.W. Chanter, C.L. Robertson, and H.S. Day.
Officers (1901–3)	Traffic Manager: Henry Sowden. Resident Engineer: W.J. Gale. Chief Engineer & Consultant: Stephen Sellon.
Head Offices	Bideford: 20, The Quay, (BWH&AR Company Office). London: Donington House, Norfolk Street, The Strand, London WC (Head Office of the British Electric Traction Company, which owned the BWH&AR).
Date of Closure	27th March, 1917.

Bideford Bridge, with East-the-Water to the right and Bideford itself to the left of the picture. *Oakwood Collection*

A turn-of-the-century view of Bideford Quay, from an Edwardian coloured postcard.
Oakwood Collection

Bideford Quay, looking south towards the bridge from the BWH&AR terminus during the early 1900s.
Oakwood Collection

Chapter One
Origins of the Bideford, Westward Ho! & Appledore Railway

The sea has, for many centuries, been a dominant factor in British history and British life, and it is clearly no coincidence that most of England's oldest towns and cities were also sea ports. One thinks, for example, of London, Bristol and Exeter – all of which were regarded as important places in Medieval times. Most towns of any significance were situated on the coast or on navigable waterways such as the Thames or Severn, and in an age when decent roads simply did not exist, it is hardly surprising that the nation's goods and merchandise were transported primarily by river or coastal transport. As navigational methods became more sophisticated, little ships began to venture beyond the confines of Britain's coastal waters, and by the middle of the 16th century long-distance ocean voyages had become almost commonplace.

In the Tudor period, England became conscious of its unique position as an island nation on the very edge of Europe, and Elizabethan sailors and adventurers such as Sir Walter Raleigh (1552–1618), Sir Richard Grenville (1540–1591) and Sir Francis Drake (1540–1596) ranged the oceans of the world in their small, but sturdy sailing vessels. Many of these adventurers came from the West Country – Devon, in particular, being a veritable breeding ground for Elizabethan seafarers.

It is unclear why Devon should have produced so many Elizabethan sea captains, though the facts of geography must have played an important part in the process whereby West Country ports such as Plymouth and Bristol were able to develop a profitable trans-Atlantic trade with the new lands on the far side of the ocean. At the same time, it is conceivable that the legacy of ancient Celtic landowning systems contributed to the growth of large numbers of impoverished gentry in Devon and Cornwall; farms and estates were much smaller than in other parts of England, and this meant that personal fortunes were unlikely to have been made in agriculture. Instead, men such as Drake and Raleigh opted for somewhat more adventurous careers on the high seas – and their home ports became centres of intense activity as ships were fitted out for the long and perilous voyages to the new and distant lands across the seas.

Bideford & Appledore

Bideford, a small town and port on the River Torridge in north Devon, was the ancestral home of the Grenvilles. The manor of Bideford had been granted to one Sir Richard de Granvill by King William Rufus, and the Grenvilles resided in Devon for many generations. In 1585 Sir Richard Grenville returned from the island of Roanoke, off the coast of Carolina, bringing with him the first native American Indian to visit England, while three years later Bideford sent five ships to fight the Spanish Armada.

In 1591, Sir Richard Grenville's ship, the *Revenge* – crewed largely by Bideford men – was one of a small English squadron sent to intercept a Spanish treasure fleet off the Azores. This small force was itself surprised by a much larger Spanish fleet of 53 ships, but Grenville sailed the *Revenge* straight at the enemy ships, and managed to sink at least two of them in a courageous, but entirely one-sided battle. In the end Grenville, mortally wounded, ordered his men to blow up the Revenge, but (perhaps understandably) the surviving English sailors preferred to surrender. The gallant Revenge was sunk in a storm which swept the Azores in the next few days, and in this way Sir Richard Grenville's last fight passed into English history – and Grenville thereby became Bideford's greatest local hero.

By 1680, Bideford had emerged as one of the most important trans-Atlantic ports in England – only London and Topsham having a larger share of the growing trade with Virginia and Maryland. The main product imported at that time was tobacco, though many local vessels were engaged in the highly profitable Newfoundland cod trade.

Seventeenth century Bideford was a small, but bustling sea port, and a contemporary topographer described this North Devon town as follows. It was, he wrote:

> ... Famous for the resort of people to it, and for its arched stone bridge. This is so high that a ship of fifty or sixty tons may sail under it. For which, and for the number of its arches, it equals, if not exceeds, all others in England. It was begun by Sir Thoebald Granvill; and, for the finishing of it, the Bishop of the Diocese granted out indulgences to move the people to liberal contribution; and, accordingly, great sums of money were collected.
>
> This place hath been in the possession of the Greenvills ever since the conquest; a family famous for Sir Richard Greenvill's behaviour in Glamorganshire, in the reign of William Rufus, and for another of the same name under Queen Elizabeth who, with one ship, maintained a sea-fight for twenty four hours, against fifty of the Spanish galleons; and, at last, yielded upon honourable terms, after his powder was spent, having slain above one thousand of the Spaniards, and sunk four of their vessels.[1]

Bideford continued to prosper throughout the 18th century, and Daniel Defoe, who visited the town in the 1740s, was much impressed by the well-built merchants' houses which he found in Bridgeland Street. This thoroughfare was, he claimed, as 'broad as the High Street in Exeter, well-built, and which is more than all, well-inhabited with considerable and wealthy merchants who trade to most parts of the world'.

Appledore, some two miles downstream from Bideford, was said to have been a 'good village' during the early 16th century, and in the ensuing years this village developed as both a port and a shipbuilding centre. The history of Appledore was, in many ways, similar to that of neighbouring Bideford; both of these ports flourished during the 17th and 18th centuries, but as ships became bigger Appledore's trade increased at the expense of Bideford. Both ports were, nevertheless, busy during the Victorian period when large numbers of local vessels were engaged in the coastal, Irish and Spanish trades.

In the meantime, Appledore had achieved even greater prominence as a ship building centre, and in Victorian times local builders such as Robert Cock, Thomas Green, William Clibbet, Arthur Cook, William Pickhard, J. Westacott and William Yeo were building or repairing large numbers of ketches, schooners, and brigantines.

Origins of the Victorian Tourist Industry

Holidays and tourism, as we know them today, were essentially a Victorian innovation. In earlier years only the very rich could afford to take holidays, but by the 19th century a growing middle class meant that seaside holidaymaking became more of a mass activity. Small 'resorts' such as Torquay, Cromer and Hastings began to develop, while certain other seaside towns – notably Blackpool, Southport and Morecambe – were turned into fashionable residential towns from which Victorian businessmen commuted to distant industrial centres such as Leeds and Bradford. Elsewhere, landowners and entrepreneurs such as Sir Peter Hesketh Fleetwood and Henry le Strange laid out planned holiday resorts such as Fleetwood and New Hunstanton, and significant fortunes were made as these new resort developments mushroomed into bustling seaside towns.

There were, in fact, several types of Victorian holiday town. Some resorts were both holiday centres and residential towns, while others gained reputations as 'health' resorts for invalids or retired people. Other (usually smaller) towns or villages catered for lovers of the quaint and picturesque, and in this context West Country towns and villages such as St Ives, Lynmouth and Clovelly were able to develop without losing their essential character.

Bideford and Appledore were both 'discovered' by middle class holidaymakers during the 19th century – although it should be stressed that these two North Devon ports continued to function as commercial trading and ship building centres throughout the 19th and early 20th centuries. There was, at the same time, an influx of summer visitors into the area, and this annual invasion of summer tourists was caused, in great part, by the interest and enthusiasm of Charles Kingsley (1819–1875), and his famous seafaring novel *Westward Ho!*.

The Influence of Charles Kingsley

Born in Devon, Charles Kingsley embodied much of what was good in the Victorian age. A great scholar, his interests were wide-ranging, though he might best be described as a poet, reformer, novelist and Anglican clergyman.[2] His published works encompassed both social issues and historical romance, and like many Victorians this 'Christian Socialist' thinker managed to combine socialism with an unshakable belief in England's greatness as a bastion of liberal, Protestant values.

Published in 1855, *Westward Ho!* was one of Charles Kingsley's earliest novels, but it encapsulated many of his deepest beliefs vis-à-vis Devonshire history, Protestantism, and the struggle waged against Catholic Spain. The tale of Amyas Leigh – a Bideford sea captain – the book combined both fact and fiction; real life characters such as Sir Richard Grenville mingled with fictional creations such as Amyas Leigh and Salvation Yeo, and the story was firmly set in real life locations such as Bideford and Appledore. The narrative was redolent of Devon, the Tudor Age and the sea, while for Victorian readers this epic tale of adventure and exploration had a special significance in that it recalled the birth of the British Empire – the very name, *Westward Ho!* seemed to conjure up visions of Devonshire ships setting their prows towards distant, unclaimed lands beyond the seas.

The Creation of Westward Ho!

The new novel was an instant success, and its fame inevitably brought fresh visitors to the quaint old sea-faring towns of Bideford and Appledore. Meanwhile, in a simultaneous development, a local property company had built the first houses in an entirely new resort development on the unspoiled stretch of coast to the west of Appledore. Promoted by the Northam Burrows Hotel & Villa Company, this new settlement was, from its inception, an entirely speculative affair; it was hoped that a populous seaside resort would grow up within sight of the famous natural feature known as Pebble Ridge, and the scheme's supporters hoped that this Victorian resort development would bring increased prosperity to the surrounding area. Golf enthusiasts were expected to form a large proportion of the new town's patrons, and to achieve this aim the Royal North Devon Golf Club was formed in 1863, with attractive golf links (one of the first in the country) on the open 'Burrows' behind Pebble Ridge.

As first projected the new seaside town would presumably have been named 'Northam Burrows', but, noting the immense success of Charles Kingsley's novel, the Northam Burrows Hotel & Villa Company decided to call their resort 'Westward Ho!'. Ironically, Kingsley was unimpressed by this new venture, and he was by no means happy about the chosen name. In 1864 he wrote the following letter to a friend:

> How goes on the Northam Burrows scheme for spoiling that beautiful place with hotels and villas? I suppose it must be, but you will frighten away all the sea-pies and defile the Pebble Ridge with chicken bones and sandwich scraps. The universe is growing cockney, and men like me must look out for a new planet to live in, without fear of railways and villa projections.[3]

Charles Kingsley's reference to 'fear of railways' is particularly significant in respect to new seaside developments, insofar as no resorts could have grown up without the railways. In a sense, all Victorian holiday resorts were railway creations in that the railways made transport both cheap and efficient, not only for goods traffic but also for large numbers of ordinary people. Railways were fast and (compared to the earlier stage coaches) cheap to travel on, and it would be true to say that most, if not all, 19th century resort promoters were also firm supporters of new railway schemes. At Hunstanton, for example, Henry Le Strange realised that his projected seaside town needed a rail link to the outside world, and the Lynn & Hunstanton Railway was therefore launched in order to bring holiday-makers to the new resort.[4] Similarly, Morecambe in Lancashire was closely linked to the Morecambe Bay Harbour & Railway Company, while Fleetwood could not have been founded as a new port and town without the Preston & Wyre Railway, Dock & Harbour Company.

In the case of Westward Ho! the link between railways and resort development was equally important – although in this case it could be argued that the *lack* of suitable railway connections impeded the rapid growth of the town. There were, on the other hand, plans for a rail link to Bideford and Westward Ho! which, if successfuly completed, would have transformed the character of the growing resort out of all recognition; but before examining these abortive plans in greater detail it is necessary, first of all, to sketch in some general details regarding the origins of railways in the Bideford area.

Early Railway Schemes

Railway development in the North Devon area can be traced back to the Railway Mania years of the middle 1840s, when a variety of schemes were promoted with the aim of linking Bideford, Barnstaple and Exeter. One of the first of these schemes was the grandly-named Taw Vale Railway Extension & Dock Company, which hoped to link Exeter to Barnstaple, Ilfracombe and South Molton. This scheme – which had originated as a somewhat nebulous project back in the 1830s – was eventually taken up by the London & South Western Railway, and with Joseph Locke (1805–1860) as its Engineer, the Taw Vale Railway appeared to have an assured future as a branch of the LSWR.

Another scheme suggested at this time was the North Devon Railway. The North Devon promoters hoped to build a line running westwards from Tiverton, through Bampton, Dulverton and Barnstaple to Bideford, with a possible branch from Barnstaple to Ilfracombe. The North Devon project was backed by the Great Western Railway, and with Isambard Kingdom Brunel (1806–1859) as its Engineer the line was to be built on the GWR broad gauge of 7 ft 0¼ in. Meanwhile, other interests were actively promoting the rival Cornwall & Devon Central Railway between Exeter, Okehampton, Bodmin and Falmouth, while a further scheme envisaged a branch from Bideford to Okehampton.

These diverse schemes came before Parliament in the session of 1847, but all of them were thrown out with the exception of the Taw Vale scheme. There had, in the interim, been a significant change of plan in that the Taw Vale Railway was now seen as a line from Barnstaple to Crediton – the intervening section between Exeter and Crediton being filled by a separate company.

Unfortunately, the boom years of the Railway Mania were followed by a severe trade depression. This was, at least in part, because far too much money had been wasted in needless speculation, but at the same time, bad harvests from the end of 1845 until 1849 had thrown the Victorian financial system into chaos. The continued economic crisis led to riots and revolutions throughout Europe, and in these unhappy circumstances the railway stock market collapsed in its entirety.

Most of the wild schemes hatched during the Mania years were abandoned, and established companies such as the GWR and the LSWR were themselves obliged to reduce expenditure on new lines. One of the victims of this economic crisis was the Taw Vale Railway which, by 1848, had been reduced to little more than a tramway between Fremington and

Barnstaple; the line was worked entirely by horses as a goods-only route, and there were no connections to any other railway.

Improved trading conditions in the early 1850s led to a revival of interest in the proposed rail link from Exeter to Bideford, and after many vicissitudes a line was finally completed between Exeter and Barnstaple. This line was owned by two broad gauge companies; the Exeter & Crediton Railway and the North Devon Railway. Both of these eventually passed into London & South Western ownership although, as a result of earlier alliances, LSWR trains had to run over the rival Great Western system in order to reach the Barnstaple line at Cowley Bridge Junction, north of Exeter.

The Exeter & Crediton Railway had been opened first, on 12th May, 1851. Completion throughout to Barnstaple followed on 1st August, 1854, when the North Devon line was opened from Crediton to Barnstaple (confusingly, the North Devon company was in fact the Taw Vale Railway & Dock Company, which had changed its name by an Act of 24th July, 1851).

There was, as yet, no direct rail link from Barnstaple to Bideford, but on 4th August, 1853, the Bideford Extension Railway was empowered to construct a line along the southern side of the Taw and Torridge estuaries between Barnstaple, Fremington and a station at East-the-Water, near Bideford bridge. This line would incorporate the existing freight-only line between Barnstaple and Fremington, which would be upgraded for use by passenger trains to and from Bideford with broad gauge trackwork to accommodate the 7 ft gauge North Devon trains from Barnstaple.

The Bideford Extension line was substantially complete by the closing months of 1855, and the route was ceremonially opened for the carriage of passengers on Monday 29th October, 1855. Regular services commenced on 2nd November, 1855, with an initial train service of five trains in each direction to and from Bideford – most of them running through to Exeter.[6]

The Bideford Extension line provided useful transport facilities for people living in the Bideford and Appledore areas, but there were still hopes that further lines could also be built from Bideford to Torrington, and from Bideford to the growing resort of Westward Ho!. Accordingly, in the middle 1860s, two branch line schemes were promoted, one of which – the Torrington Extension Railway – sought Powers to extend the Bideford branch southwards to Torrington, while the other hoped to secure the desired rail link between Bideford, Appledore & Westward Ho!.

The Torrington scheme was first in the field, having obtained its Act on 19th June, 1865. The line would, in effect, be a branch of the London & South Western Railway, and the LSWR company was authorised to spend £80,000 on the construction of this five and a half mile line. The Bideford to Appledore line, in contrast, was an independent scheme, and as this project was the immediate predecessor of the Bideford, Westward Ho! & Appledore Railway it would be appropriate to examine the original 1860s proposals in detail.

The Bideford, Appledore & Westward Ho! Railway

Unlike the Torrington Extension line, which was seen as an extension of the existing Bideford branch, the proposed Bideford, Appledore & Westward

Ho! Railway would have been a completely isolated line on the western side of the River Torridge. The Appledore scheme was presented to Parliament in the 1866 session, and on 16th July, 1866, the Act 'For making a railway from Bideford to Appledore, with a branch to Westward Ho! in the County of Devon' received the Royal Assent.[5]

The Bideford, Appledore & Westward Ho! Act (29 & 30 Vic. cap. 224) provided consent for a two mile railway from Bideford to Appledore, and a branch of similar length to Westward Ho!, the total length of line authorised by the 1866 Act being four miles. These two lines were carefully defined, and for ease of reference they were designated Railway Number One and Railway Number Two. Railway Number One (the main line) was described as:

> A Railway two miles and 4.20 chains in length . . . commencing at a point in a field called Hogg's Marsh, belonging to Thomas Diamond and Howard Effingham Hogg, or one of them, in the Parish of Northam, and numbered 1 on the Tithe Apportionment Map of the said parish, being about four chains measured at right angles eastward across the said field from a point on the fence dividing the same from field number 2, six chains and ninety links or thereabouts distant from the north-western corner, and terminating at or near Appledore at a point on the beach or foreshore in the said Parish of Northam, belonging to Mr William Yeo and in his occupation; which said point is at the south-west angle of, and abuts upon, an enclosure in the said parish belonging to Mr William Yeo, and occupied by Mr William Clibbett, and numbered 1,039 on the said map; which said line of railway, and the stations, approaches, and works belonging thereto, will be situate and pass, or be made in or through, the several parishes and places of Bideford, Northam and East and West Appledore, or some or one of them in the County of Devon.

From this main line the branch would diverge westwards to reach Westward Ho! at a point on the coast near Rock Nose, the exact route of the line being defined as:

> A Railway one mile 7 furlongs and 2.80 chains in length (herein called Railway Number Two) to Westward Ho! near Rock Nose, commencing by a junction with Railway Number One in a field numbered 865 on the Tithe Apportionment Map of the Parish of Northam, belonging to Mr William Yeo and occupied by Mr James Partridge, and terminating in a field belonging to and occupied by the Northam Burrows Hotel and Villa Company Limited, numbered 606 on the said map, at or near a point distant three chains or thereabouts measured along its western boundary from the fence dividing it from the enclosure No. 607 on the said map, such enclosure forming the lawn in front of Youngston Farm House, the whole of which said railway Number Two will pass, or be made in or through, the said parishes and places of Northam, and East and West Appledore, or one of them, in the said County of Devon.

To pay for this scheme the promoters were authorised to raise £60,000 'in six thousand shares of ten pounds each'. Sadly, the sudden failure of bankers Overend & Gurney in May 1866 had resulted in another economic crisis, and with the bank rate standing at 10 per cent small companies such as the newly-incorporated Bideford, Appledore & Westward Ho! Railway were unable to raise their authorised capital.

Undaunted by this major setback to their modest, but entirely feasible plans, the Bideford, Appledore & Westward Ho! promoters struggled on for several more years. In the end, however, the disappointed Westward Ho! supporters were forced to admit defeat, and their scheme was abandoned in its entirety. In the meantime the supporters of the Torrington scheme had faced similar problems in the aftermath of the 1866 financial crisis. Little had been done towards implementing this scheme, but finally (after two attempts to abandon the project) the LSWR began constructing the Torrington Extension Railway in 1870.

The new line was inspected by Colonel Yolland of the Board of Trade in June 1872, and on Monday 10th June, 1871 the Torrington line was finally opened to public traffic. In conjunction with this scheme, a new station was constructed at Bideford East-the-Water for passenger traffic, and the old station became an enlarged goods depot. The new station was better situated in relation to Bideford proper, being directly opposite the eastern end of Bideford bridge.

The successful completion of the Torrington scheme must have given encouragement to those who still hoped that Appledore and Westward Ho! could be served by a direct rail link. One of the most enthusiastic supporters of a railway from Bideford to Westward Ho! was Captain George Frederick Molesworth RN of Westward Ho!, while local landowners such as George T. Taylor of Abbotsham Court were also keen to see the advantages of rail transport brought to Westward Ho!.

There were, at various times, hopes that the London & South Western Railway could be persuaded to build such a line – perhaps by means of a bridge across the River Torridge at Bideford or some other convenient place. The LSWR had, it is true, tightened its grip on the North Devon line, having acquired control of this important route from pro-GWR interests, and then progressively converted it to the standard gauge of 4 ft 8½ in. In this context it may be worth adding that the Torrington extension line had been a standard gauge route from its inception, whereas the earlier line between Barnstaple and Bideford retained its mixed gauge trackwork until the 1870s.

In reality, the London & South Western Railway had little interest in the area beyond Bideford; the existing facilities between Bideford and Torrington provided a perfectly adequate passenger and goods service for local residents and traders, and with extensive carrier and omnibus services readily available to and from Bideford station, the LSWR clearly felt that further extensions would be superfluous. If, on the other hand, an independent company was prepared to spend money on new lines the London & South Western Railway would clearly have welcomed any extra traffic that might have been generated – the South Western company had no objection to extensions as such, but it had no wish to squander its own money on schemes that would, at best, be marginally profitable.

Light Railway Schemes

It was, by the 1890s, clear to all concerned that if Westward Ho! was to have its own railway the project would have to be undertaken by a locally-based company. The amount of passenger and freight traffic that would be generated by such a line was likely to be small, but Captain Molesworth and his fellow promoters realised that if construction costs could be kept to a minimum their scheme could yet be implemented.

There was, in the second half of the 19th century, much debate on the subject of railway construction in rural areas. Rural depopulation had become a major issue, especially in remote and backward parts of the United Kindgom such as the south and west of Ireland and the Highlands of Scotland. To mitigate this problem successive governments had introduced a variety of Acts that attempted to simplify the system whereby railways were built. The Railway Construction Facilities Act of 1864, for example, had enabled promoters to build lines in cases where all of the landowners concerned had agreed to the proposals. Four years later, in 1868, The Regulation of Railways Act enabled the Board of Trade to grant licences to railway companies authorising them to build and work as light railways any part of the lines that those companies had Powers to construct and work.

In Ireland, meanwhile, a whole series of Acts (such as the Relief & Distress Amendment Act of 1880) had enabled railways to be constructed with help from local authorities. Moreover, the promoters of these Irish lines were able to obtain an Order in Council instead of a more expensive Act of Parliament – the whole system of light railway promotion being designed to bring down costs to such an extent that private enterprise would provide much needed infrastructure in remote and distressed areas.

In a further development, many lines in Ireland and elsewhere were built on the narrow gauge of three feet (or less), and this expedient enabled further economies to be introduced on lines that were already much cheaper than comparable standard gauge railways.

On 14th August, 1896, Parliament passed a further light railway Act with the specific aim of 'facilitating the construction of light railways' which would be 'found beneficial to the rural districts'. The Light Railways Act of 1896 was, in effect, a logical culmination of the various light railway and tramway Acts passed between 1864 and 1883. Like its predecessors, the 1896 Act made railway construction much easier and cheaper; the new Act was similar to the earlier Irish Acts in that it enabled local and national government assistance to be made available to the promoters of light railways who (instead of obtaining an expensive Act of Parliament) would be able to apply for a much cheaper Light Railway Order.

The new system was facilitated by the creation of three Light Railway Commissioners, who were appointed by the Board of Trade to administer the scheme. The Commissioners were given powers to grant Light Railway Orders in approved cases, although these Orders could, if necessary, be rejected by the Board of Trade. If local authorities agreed to subscribe to lines in their respective areas, the Treasury was able to arrange loans of up to 25 per cent of the required capital, provided that 50 per cent of the capital was share capital subscribed for in the normal way.

The most important aspect of the new scheme, as far as the Westward Ho! promoters were concerned, was the fact that light railway procedures were destined to become much cheaper and simpler in the sense that normal Board of Trade regulations were considerably relaxed. Signalling arrangements, for example, could be reduced to the barest minimum (or dispensed with altogether) while level crossing gates, platform shelters and a whole range of other refinements were no longer an absolute necessity on lightly-built lines in remote rural areas.

The new light railway legislation – which had first been brought to public notice in the Queen's Speech of 1895 – was a synthesis of many existing procedures. It was an example of evolution rather than revolution, but the passage of the new Light Railway Bill was nevertheless followed with interest by the promoters of rural lines throughout the country. Those who had argued for new railways (and other infrastructure) to stem the tide of rural depopulation in distressed areas were particularly pleased with the provisions enshrined in the Light Railways Act, and when the new Bill was passed light railway schemes enjoyed renewed popularity in a number of areas that had not, hitherto, been served directly by rail transport.

The Formation of the Bideford, Westward Ho! & Appledore Railway

Westward Ho! was hardly a distressed area, but with light and narrow gauge railways being constructed in increasing numbers in Ireland and in other parts of the United Kingdom the supporters of the Westward Ho! scheme agreed that their needs would best be served by the formation of a light railway or tramway company. The Light Railways Act of 1896 had not yet been passed, but earlier legislation such as the Regulation of Railways Act 1868 had already provided scope for the construction of a light railway.

To reduce costs further, the promoters decided that part of their line would be built as a street tramway, while even greater economies could be achieved if the proposed light railway or tramway was constructed as a narrow gauge line.

If the line to Westward Ho! was built as a narrow gauge route there would be no need to provide a direct connection with the LSWR station at Bideford East-the-Water, and for this reason the promoters saw no need to build an expensive bridge across the River Torridge. As in 1866, the proposed line would be entirely self-contained, the idea being that the railway would commence on the west side of Bideford bridge and then proceed more or less due west along the Kenwith Valley to the coast at Cornborough Cliffs. From Cornborough, the route would continue along the coast to Westward Ho!, and thence north-eastwards to a terminus at Appledore.

It was calculated that such a line could be constructed and opened for around £50,000, and the provisional capital of the Bideford, Westward Ho! & Appledore Railway was accordingly fixed at £50,000 in £10 shares.

Before commencing work on the proposed railway the Bideford, Westward Ho! & Appledore promoters had first to obtain an Act of Parliament, and in 1895 Captain Molesworth, George Taylor and the other promoters started preparing their scheme for submission to Parliament in the coming session.

On 17th February, 1896 George Mill, Frederick Molesworth and George Taylor formally petitioned Parliament for leave to bring in a Bill incorporating 'The Bideford, Westward Ho! & Appledore Railway', and the petition having been presented and read, the Bill itself was read for the first time 'and ordered to be read a second time', on 18th February.[7]

The Bideford, Westward Ho! & Appledore Railway Bill was read for the third time on 11th March, 1896, and in compliance with standard Parliamentary procedures the Clerk was then ordered to carry the Bill up to the Lords.

On 17th March the *Journal of the House of Lords* reported that the Westward Ho! Bill had been brought from the Commons and read for the first time in the Upper House. The Bill was read for the second time by the Lords on 26th March, after which it was 'committed to the consideration of the Chairman of Committees'.

Having passed this final hurdle the scheme received its third reading in the Upper House on 27th April, 1896; the Lords Committee had, by that time, introduced certain very minor amendments regarding the operation of the line as a light railway, but none of these changes were of a controversial nature, and after being returned to the House of Commons for further perusal the 'Act for incorporating the Bideford, Westward Ho! & Appledore Railway Company' received the Royal Assent on 21st May, 1896.[8]

Having obtained their Act, the Bideford, Westward Ho! & Appledore Railway supporters were able to organise themselves into a properly constituted company with its own Chairman and Board of Directors, and as the spring of 1896 turned to summer the people of Westward Ho! and the surrounding area were at last able to look ahead to the day when their thriving resort would be connected by rail to the neighbouring towns of Bideford and Appledore.

On a footnote, it is interesting to note that the Bideford, Westward Ho! & Appledore Railway was only one of a number of light railway schemes promoted during the middle 1890s. Like the BWH&AR project, many of these schemes actually *predated* the 1896 Light Railways Act, and one wonders, in fact, why their promoters could not have waited just a few more months in order to take full advantage of the new legislation. The likeliest answer to this question is probably connected with the publicity surrounding the Light Railways Act – quite simply, railway promoters would have read about the proposed new legislation long before the Act was finally passed, and this would, in turn, have given greater credence to the whole concept of light railway construction.

(Once the Light Railways Act had been passed, railway promoters were of course able to take full advantage of it, and, as we shall see, the BWH&AR route was belatedly completed under the terms of a Light Railway Order, as provided for in the Light Railways Act of 1896.)

AN

A C T

[ROYAL ASSENT 21ST MAY 1896.]

For incorporating the Bideford Westward Ho! and Appledore Railway Company and for other purposes.

WHEREAS the construction of the Railway or Tramway and Railways hereinafter described in the county of Devon would be of public and local advantage: *Preamble.*

And whereas the several persons hereinafter named with 5 others are willing at their own expense to carry the undertaking by this Act authorised into execution on being incorporated into a Company for the purpose:

And whereas it is expedient that the powers in this Act contained relative to the providing by the Company of hotels and

Some extracts from the Bideford, Westward Ho! & Appledore Railway Act of 21st May, 1896.

4   *The Bideford Westward Ho! and Appledore Railway Act* 1896.

conveniences connected therewith and may enter upon take and use such of the lands delineated on the said plans and described in the deposited books of reference as may be required for that purpose.

The Railway hereinbefore referred to and authorised by this Act is—

A Railway or Tramway (No. 1) one furlong nine chains and fifty links in length of which three chains is double line and one furlong six chains and fifty links is single line commencing in the parish and borough of Bideford in the centre of the street running alongside of and parallel with the quay at Bideford aforesaid at a point twelve yards or thereabouts measured in a northerly direction from an imaginary line extended from the westernmost end of the bridge known as Bideford Bridge and in a line with the northern parapet of that bridge to the centre of the roadway of such street and terminating in the said parish and borough of Bideford at a point five yards or thereabouts measured in an easterly direction from the north-east corner and in line with the north face of the building known as the Municipal Technical School at Bideford;

A Railway (No. 2) four miles three furlongs nine chains and ninety links in length commencing at the point of termination of the said Railway or Tramway No. 1 and terminating in the parish of Northam at a point seventy-nine yards or thereabouts measured in a northerly direction along the west side of the roadway leading from Nelson Terrace to the Pebbleridge at Westward Ho! in the said parish of Northam from an imaginary line drawn from the north-west corner and in line with the north front of the said Nelson Terrace;

A Railway (No. 3) two miles three furlongs and 4·20 chains in length commencing at the point of termination of Railway No. 2 and terminating in the said parish of Northam at a point twenty yards or thereabouts from

The Bideford Westward Ho! and Appledore Railway Act 1896. 5

the north-west corner of the national school at Appledore measured in a westerly direction in line with the north face of the said school house.

6. Subject to the provisions in this Act contained as to the Railway or Tramway No. 1 by this Act authorised and to the provisions of Sections 28 and 29 of the Regulation of Railways Act 1868 the Railway may if so resolved by the Directors of the Company be constructed and worked as a light Railway. *Railway may be a light Railway.*

7. The Railway shall be made and maintained on a gauge of three feet Provided that it shall be lawful for the Company at any time hereafter with the previous approval of the Board of Trade to increase the gauge from three feet to any gauge not exceeding four feet eight and a-half inches Provided further that so much of Section thirty-four of the Tramways Act 1870 as limits the extent of the carriage used on any tramway beyond the outer edge of the wheels of such carriage shall not apply to carriages used on the Railway. *Gauge of Railway.*

8. The capital of the Company shall be fifty thousand pounds in five thousand shares of ten pounds each. *Capital*

9. The Company shall not issue any share created under the authority of this Act nor shall any such share vest in the person or corporation accepting the same unless and until a sum not being less than one-fifth of the amount of such share is paid in respect thereof. *Shares not to be issued until one-fifth paid.*

10. One-fifth of the amount of a share shall be the greatest amount of a call and two months at least shall be the interval between successive calls and three-fourths of the amount of a share shall be the utmost aggregate amount of the calls made in any year upon any share. *Calls.*

11. If any money is payable to a shareholder or mortgagee or debenture stockholder being a minor idiot or lunatic the receipt of *Receipt in case of persons not sui juris.*

The Bideford Westward Ho! and Appledore Railway Act 1896. 35

For any parcel exceeding fifty-six pounds but not exceeding five hundred pounds the Company may demand any sum they think fit.

Provided always that articles sent in large aggregate quantities although made up in separate parcels such as bags of sugar coffee meal and the like shall not be deemed small parcels but that term shall apply only to single parcels in separate packages.

46. The maximum rate of charge to be made by the Company for the conveyance of passengers upon the Railway including every expense incidental to such conveyance shall not exceed the following (that is to say) :— Maximum rates for conveyance of passengers.

For every passenger conveyed in a first-class carriage three pence per mile;

For every passenger conveyed in a second-class carriage two pence per mile;

For every passenger conveyed in a third-class carriage one penny per mile;

For every passenger conveyed on the Railway for a less distance than four miles the Company may charge as for four miles and every fraction of a mile beyond four miles or any greater number of miles shall be deemed a mile.

47. Every passenger travelling upon the Railway may take with him his ordinary luggage not exceeding one hundred and twenty pounds in weight for first-class passengers one hundred pounds in weight for second-class passengers and sixty pounds in weight for third-class passengers without any charge being made for the carriage thereof. Passengers' luggage.

48. The restrictions as to the charges to be made for passengers shall not extend to any special train run upon the Railway in respect of which the Company may make such charges Foregoing charges not to apply to special trains.

An atmospheric scene on Appledore's picturesque quay, probably photographed during the 1880s.

Rob Dark Collection

Chapter Two
Construction, Opening and Early Years of the Westward Ho! Line

The Bideford, Westward Ho! & Appledore Railway Act of 1896 provided consent for the construction of seven miles of railway, with 'all proper stations, sidings, approaches, works and conveniences connected therewith'. Five years were allowed for completion of the works, and the authorised capital of the Bideford, Westward Ho! & Appledore company was 'fifty thousand pounds in five thousand shares of ten pounds each'.

Some Details of the 1896 Act of Parliament

As in 1866, the route of the proposed railway was very carefully defined, and for ease of reference the authorised Bideford, Westward Ho! & Appledore line was treated as three distinct railways.

Railway Number One, which would be situated entirely within the Borough of Bideford, would in fact be a street tramway. This part of the BWH&AR line was defined as follows:

> A Railway or Tramway (No. 1) one furlong nine chains and fifty lines in length, of which three chains is double line and one furlong six chains and fifty links is single line, commencing in the Parish and Borough of Bideford in the centre of the street running alongside of and parallel with the quay at Bideford aforesaid at a point twelve yards or thereabouts measured in a northerly direction from an imaginary line extended from the westernmost end of the bridge known as Bideford Bridge and in line with the northern parapet of that bridge to the centre of the roadway of such street, and terminating in the said Parish and Borough of Bideford at a point five yards or thereabouts measured in an easterly direction from the north-east corner and in line with the north face of the building known as the Municipal Technical School at Bideford.

The next section of line, described as Railway Number Two, would extend from the Technical School at Bideford to the coast at Westward Ho!. This line, some 4 miles 39 chains in length, was defined as:

> A Railway (No. 2) four miles three furlongs nine chains and ninety links in length, commencing at the point of termination of the said Railway or Tramway No. 1 and terminating in the Parish of Northam at a point seventy nine yards or thereabouts measured in a northerly direction along the west side of the roadway leading from Nelson Terrace to the Pebble Ridge at Westward Ho! in the said Parish of Northam from an imaginary line drawn from the north-west corner and in line with the north front of the said Nelson Terrace.

Finally, a third section of line, known as Railway Number Three, would continue for a further 2 miles 34 chains from Westward Ho! to Appledore. Railway Number Three was described as a railway:

> Two miles three furlongs and 4.20 chains in length commencing at the point of termination of Railway No. 2 and terminating in the said Parish of Northam at a point twenty yards or thereabouts from the north-west corner of the national school at Appledore measured in a westerly direction in line with the north face of the said school house.

George Frederick Molesworth, George James Taylor, and Charles Eagle Bott were mentioned by name as the first Directors of the Bideford,

Westward Ho! & Appledore Railway Company, and these gentlemen were to remain in office until the first general meeting of the shareholders; at that meeting, the assembled proprietors would be permitted to elect a new body of Directors, or so many new Directors as were necessary to replace those Directors not continuing in office.

Further provisions dealt with the gauge of the railway, and in this context it is interesting to note that the Act allowed the promoters to construct and maintain their line 'on a gauge of three feet', with the proviso that – subject to Board of Trade approval – it would be 'lawful for the Company at any time . . . to increase the gauge from three feet to any gauge not exceeding four feet eight and a half inches'.

Another clause permitted the Directors of the Bideford, Westward Ho! & Appledore Railway to work the line as a light railway, the relevant section of the Act being as follows:

> Subject to the provisions in this Act contained as to the Railway or Tramway No. 1 by this Act authorised, and to the provisions of sections 28 and 29 of the Regulation of Railways Act 1868, the railway may, if so resolved by the Directors of the Company, be constructed and worked as a light railway.

There were certain complications in respect of the street tramway section on Bideford Quay, and for this reason the Act contained an additional clause relating to the use of 'animal, electric or mechanical power' on Railway Number One. The following extract, with its contorted wording, was destined to cause some confusion in the minds of certain local councillors – some of whom claimed that the quayside tramway at Bideford could only be worked by horses. In reality, the Act stated that mechanical or electric power *could* be employed subject to Board of Trade approval, although this point was, to some extent, obscured by the complex sentences used in the following clause:

> The carriages used on the Tramway may, subject to the provisions of this Act, be moved by animal power, and during a period of seven years after the opening of the same for public traffic, and with the consent of the Board of Trade, during such further periods of seven years as the said Board may from time to time specify in any Order to be signed by a Secretary or an Assistant-Secretary of the said Board, by steam or electric power or such other mechanical power as may be from time to time approved by the Board of Trade; provided always that the exercise of the powers hereby conferred with respect to the use of any power other than animal power shall be subject to the regulations set forth in the Schedule to this Act annexed, and to any regulations which may be added thereto or substituted therefor respectively by any Order which the Board of Trade may, and which they are hereby empowered to make from time to time as and when they may think fit for securing to the public all reasonable protection against danger in the exercise of the powers by this Act conferred with respect to the use of any power other than animal power on the Tramways.

Other sections of the Bideford, Westward Ho! & Appledore Act dealt with the rates and charges to be made for the carriage of passenger and parcels traffic. In general, these rates and charges would be the same as those scheduled to the London & South Western Railway Company (Rates and Charges) Order Confirmation Act of 1891.

The maximum rates of charge to be made by the BWH&AR Company for the conveyance of passengers was 3d. per mile for first class passengers, 2d. per mile for second class travellers and 1d. per mile for third class passengers. Each passenger would be allowed to carry 'ordinary luggage' not exceeding 120 lb. in weight for first class passengers, 120 lb. in weight for second class passengers and 60 lb. in weight for third class travellers – though a later clause provided that none of the above restrictions would apply in the case of special trains.

The newly-authorised Bideford, Westward Ho! & Appledore line was, in many ways, a curious project in that it hoped to link Bideford and Appledore – a distance of only two miles – by means of a devious route that meandered across open country for no less than seven miles! This apparent eccentricity could, at least in part, be explained by the fact that the railway was closely connected with the Northam Burrows Hotel & Villa Company. Its promoters, notably Captain Molesworth and George J. Taylor, were both concerned primarily with the transport needs of Westward Ho!. Indeed, Mr Taylor was the major landowner in the Westward Ho! area, and it was obvious that his aim was to link the growing holiday resort with Bideford in the east and Appledore, to the north-east – there would thus be two main traffic flows, with many passengers making their bookings at the principal intermediate station at Westward Ho! for short distance journeys to Bideford or to Appledore.

There was, however, *another* reason for the curious route of the Bideford, Westward Ho! & Appledore line, and that reason is of considerable interest; the Westward Ho! line was in fact just one part of a much larger scheme which, if successful, would have resulted in the creation of a whole network of railways in the North Devon area.

The Bideford & Clovelly Railway

In retrospect, it appears that Captain Molesworth, George Taylor and a group of other landowners and entrepreneurs envisaged that a 'main line' could be built from Bideford to Abbotsham, and thence along the coast to Clovelly and possibly on to Hartland. This ambitious proposal visualised a junction in the Abbotsham area, from which the authorised Bideford, Westward Ho! & Appledore line would extend north towards Westward Ho! and Appledore as a 5 mile branch. The Appledore and Clovelly lines would share a common terminus at Bideford, but otherwise the BWH&AR line would be relegated to secondary importance once the 'main line' was in operation.

Perhaps surprisingly, the Clovelly scheme enjoyed significant local support, and, in the late 1890s, there seemed no obvious reason (other than lack of money) why Messrs Molesworth and Taylor should not have been able to implement their entire scheme.

The Bideford & Clovelly Railway Bill was submitted to Parliament in the 1898 session.[9] There had, in the interim, been little attempt to proceed with the Westward Ho! scheme, although this reluctance to begin construction is understandable in view of the time and expenditure necessary in order to obtain consent for the Clovelly line. There was, nevertheless, every hope that these closely-related schemes would be able to proceed, and in March 1898 *The Railway Engineer* printed an optimistic report on the progress of what it called 'The Clovelly and Westward Ho! Railway' scheme. The Westward Ho! line was, (claimed the report) about to be started, while the Clovelly Bill was on its way through the initial stages of the Parliamentary process. The text of the report was as shown below:

> Now that the Lynton Railway is completing, the Bideford, Westward Ho! & Appledore Railway is about to be immediately commenced. At the Bideford County Sessions Mr A.J. Lawman applied for, and was granted, compulsory powers to acquire the land required for construction of the railway.
>
> Soon after Westward Ho! was brought under public notice, some fifty years ago, there was a scheme for constructing a light railway to that increasingly popular spot, but that fell through. No doubt, however, can be placed on the intention of the promoters of the present railway, as its chief financier, Mr George J. Taylor, has given his assurance that it will be commenced with the least possible delay.
>
> The contractor is Mr Charles Chadwell, well known as the constructor of tramways in London, Blackwall, Fleetwood and Dover, and his contract is for nearly £15,000. There will be three stations – one of them on Bideford Quay (for the starting point), another close to the Royal Hotel at Westward Ho! and the other at the west end of Appledore.
>
> It was intended that the railway should be a 3 ft gauge line, but that has now been altered to 4 ft 8½ in. It is expected that the railway as far as Westward Ho! will be completed in five months, and opened in June, the whole being finished by September.
>
> The Bideford–Clovelly Railway scheme is not matured as yet, but every hope is entertained that it will be made. The Act of Parliament will be applied for in the ensuing session.

On a foot note, it is interesting to note that earlier plans for the construction of a narrow gauge line appear to have been decisively rejected by the early months of 1898 – though the promoters still intended to build and operate the lines to Westward Ho! and Clovelly as cheaply-constructed light railways.

Narrow or Standard Gauge?

The question of gauge was, in fact, a major issue, with important ramifications in terms of future extensions to the LSWR at Bideford East-the-Water. A 3 ft gauge line would be relatively cheap to construct, but if this narrow gauge was adopted the Westward Ho! line could never be linked to the rest of the national railway system at Bideford (or indeed anywhere else). A 3 ft gauge line would thus remain isolated in perpetuity, and through excursions trains would never be run to Westward Ho!. If, on the other hand, the railway was built as a standard gauge line the promoters would – admittedly at some time in the distant future – still be able to link their isolated system to the London & South Western network.

There is evidence of considerable indecision in relation to the choice of gauge, but after much deliberation the Westward Ho! promoters finally opted for a 4 ft 8½ in. gauge line. Such a line would cost slightly more than a 3 ft gauge railway, but by retaining the sharp curves that would have been used on a narrow gauge line the Directors were confident that the difference in cost would not be very great. Most importantly, there would still be a chance of linking-up directly with the LSWR – one idea floated at this time being a continuation of the proposed street tramway through the streets of Bideford and across the existing road bridge to the LSWR station!

In order to alter the gauge of their authorised line the Bideford, Westward Ho! & Appledore Directors were obliged to seek Board of Trade approval, and on 30th October, 1897 the following letter was sent to the Board of Trade in London:

> Under Section Seven of the Bideford, Westward Ho! & Appledore Railway Act 1896 it is provided that the gauge of the railway should be three feet, provided that it shall be lawful for the Company at any time thereafter, with the prior consent of the Board of Trade, to increase the gauge to any gauge not exceeding 4ft 8½ inches.
>
> On going into the question of gauge, the Directors consider that it would be more advantageous to the public to construct the line, in the first instance, on the gauge of 4 ft 8½ inches, and we are directed to apply to the Board of Trade for their approval . . . the contract having been arranged, the Directors are very desirous to commence the works at once, so as to have the line ready, if possible, for next season's traffic.[10]

The Board of Trade had no objection whatsoever to the change of gauge from 3 ft to 4 ft 8½ in., but at this juncture the local authorities in Bideford commenced a campaign of obstruction and criticism that was destined to last for several years. Much of this criticism centred on the proposed use of the roadway on 'The Broad Quay' at Bideford as the site of the railway's southern terminus, and on this issue certain local politicians were determined to fight the railway every inch of the way.

Disagreement with the Borough Council

One problem, at this early stage, concerned an agreement that had previously been made between the promoters of the railway and the local council regarding the use of the quay. At a time when the gauge of the railway had not been finally chosen, the promoters had mentioned 3 ft gauge as a possible choice. Unfortunately, the local authority had assumed that 3 ft *would* be the chosen gauge, and on the basis that a narrow gauge line would take up less road space than a standard gauge railway the narrower gauge was specifically mentioned in the agreement with the local authorities. This initial agreement was, in turn, embodied in the Bideford, Westward Ho! & Appledore Railway Act of 1896, and when it became known that the Westward Ho! line was to be built as a standard gauge route local objectors were able to cite the Act in their complaints to the Board of Trade.

Having consulted their legal representatives, the objectors felt that they had a very good case, and at the end of 1897 the following solicitor's letter was sent to the Board of Trade:

> It was expressly provided by Section Four of the Act that the Company Shall not without the consent of the Corporation in writing under their seal construct that portion of Railway or Tramway Number One which lies between the point of commencement on the Broad Quay opposite the south corner of Mr Trewin's store on the Broad Quay.

As the borough Corporation had *not* given its consent in writing to the proposed change of gauge the Corporation's solicitors argued that the railway company was acting illegally; 'all that the Corporation intended to concede to the Company', added the solicitors, 'was a line of rails 3 ft across the public roadway'.

Feeling, perhaps, that they now had a strong case against the railway, the Corporation attacked the company on another issue. The authorised route of the line from Bideford Quay to Westward Ho! passed around the Bideford Technical School in a ninety degree curve, and then cut straight across an area of marshy wasteland known as 'The Pill'. Unfortunately (for the Bideford, Westward Ho! & Appledore promoters) the local authorities had acquired this riverside land by a Deed of Conveyance from the Commissioners of Woods, the intention being that a riverside garden or 'pleasure park' could be provided as a civic amenity once the Pill was properly drained.

Supporters of the 'pleasure park' idea thought that a railway running through the reclaimed 'Pill' would be an unacceptable intrusion, and in addition to their complaints vis-à-vis the quayside tramway, the Corporation also protested to the Board of Trade about the line through the Pill. It would, argued the protesters, 'be most unsightly if stations or buildings' were erected by the railway company 'on any portion of the ground'. Instead (ran the argument) the railway terminus should be banished to the very edge of the park – or else sited well away from the town at Chanter's Lane or some other discreet place on the northern side of Bideford.

Regrettably, other protesters objected to the railway being built even on the outskirts of the town, a particular objection, in this context, being the allegedly dangerous level crossings that would be required at the Causeway, Chanter's Lane and along the authorised route to Mudcott. Certain local residents added their voices to the barrage of anti-railway criticism, and in the next few weeks the Board of Trade was bombarded with letters and petitions complaining about the numerous level crossings that would be needed in the Bideford area.

It is, perhaps, highly significant that those who objected most strongly to the Bideford, Westward Ho! & Appledore Railway were primarily Bideford residents. In terms of numbers, the objectors were by no means a numerous group – but they tended to be local politicians and ratepayers who (for reasons best known to themselves) did not want the railway brought into the town of Bideford. As these individuals occupied positions of influence within the local community they were able to oppose the railway at every opportunity, and on every conceivable issue.

Many of the criticisms that had been levelled at the railway were of a petty and even spiteful nature, and one cannot escape the conclusion that personal animosities may have played at least some part in the long-running feud waged between the railway company and the local authorities. Furthermore, the Bideford faction may have felt (probably correctly) that the railway was of greater advantage to Westward Ho! than to their own town, and this lingering suspicion would have done little to reduce the mutual hostility that rapidly grew up between Bideford Corporation and the Bideford, Westward Ho! & Appledore Railway.

Meanwhile, the Bideford & Clovelly Bill – upon which many hopes were now being pinned – was progressing through Parliament, and on 25th July, 1898, the Clovelly scheme received the Royal Assent.[11]

Details of the Bideford & Clovelly Act

The resulting Act provided for the construction of a railway 10 miles 38 chains in length, which would diverge from the authorised (but as yet unbuilt) route of the Bideford, Westward Ho! & Appledore line at Kenwith Castle and terminate at Clovelly. As usual, the course of the proposed railway was clearly defined in the Act, the starting point and termination point of the line being meticulously described. The Bideford & Clovelly Railway would be a line:

> ... ten miles, three furlongs eight chains twenty links in length commencing in the Parish of Abbotsham by a junction with Railway No. 2 authorised by the Bideford, Westward Ho! and Appledore Railway Act 1896 (hereinafter called the Bideford Act) at or near a point one mile fifty two chains on the centre line of and measured from the commencement of Railway No. 2 by the said Act authorised, and terminating in the Parish of Clovelly in the County of Devon at a point three chains or thereabouts measured in a southerly direction from the Ordnance Bench Mark on the first guide post west of the ten miles stone from Bideford.

The line, of 4 ft 8½ in. gauge, could be built and worked as a light railway 'if so resolved by the Directors of the Company'.

The Bideford & Clovelly Railway had an authorised capital of £75,000 in seven thousand five hundred £10 shares, and the first Directors would be George Hill, Captain Frederick Molesworth, George John Taylor, Walter T. Ellis, and Robert William John Smart.

Five years were allowed for completion of the works, and the 1898 Act contained several provisions relating to joint operation and running powers over the Bideford, Westward Ho! & Appledore Railway between Bideford Quay and Kenwith Castle. As far as running powers were concerned, the most important section of the Act was as follows:

> The Company and any persons for the time being working or using the said railway or any part thereof may run over and use with their engines, carriages and wagons, officers and servants ... so much of the Bideford, Westward Ho! & Appledore Railway as is situate between the junction therewith of the Railway and commencement of the Railway or Tramway No. 1 by the Bideford Act authorised, including the use of stations, roads, platforms, points, signals, water, water-engines, water sheds, standing room for engines and carriages, booking and other offices, warehouses, sidings, junctions, machines, works and conveniences of or connected with the said portion of the Bideford, Westward Ho! & Appledore Railway and stations.

Although the Bideford, Westward Ho! & Appledore and Bideford & Clovelly railways would, in effect, be part of the same organisation, the Act contained provisions relating to possible disputes between the two companies. In the event of any such disputes arising the points of difference would be settled by appeal to the Board of Trade – either party having the right of appeal to this higher authority.

Construction Begins

With both Acts now obtained, the promoters were at last able to begin construction of the Westward Ho! line, and in September 1898 *The North Devon Journal* reported that 'sleepers for the Bideford, Westward Ho! & Appledore Railway' had recently been landed at Bideford. A few weeks previously, on 12th May, 1898, the same newspaper reported that 300 tons of rails had recently been delivered at Bideford Quay aboard the screw steamer *Snipe*.

Unfortunately, subsequent progress was retarded by financial and other problems, one of the worst blows at this time being a dispute which arose between the Bideford, Westward Ho! & Appledore Railway and its main contractor. Matters degenerated to such an extent that in December 1900 the contractor was removed from his post, and this resulted in protracted legal proceedings that did little to bolster the company's financial position.

With the original Bideford, Westward Ho! & Appledore scheme in difficulties, Captain Molesworth and the other promoters were unable to commence the Clovelly line, though – in anticipation that matters would soon improve – the Bideford & Clovelly Railway Company decided to prepare a new Bill seeking an extension of time to secure the requisite land. Accordingly, at the end of 1900, the necessary Bill was prepared, and on 29th December, 1900 *The Railway Times* reported that 'The Bideford & Clovelly Railway . . . had deposited a Bill for extension of time till July 1904 within which to acquire land'. At the same time, the promoters hoped to raise a further £40,333 in shares and loan capital.

The British Electric Traction Company Takeover

There had, by this time, been an important development in that the Bideford, Westward Ho! & Appledore Railway, originally an independent concern, had become a subsidiary of a much larger organisation known as The British Electric Traction Company.

As its name implied, the British Electric Traction Company was a tramway company with extensive interests in street tramways in Britain and overseas.[12] It remains a matter of conjecture why this large undertaking should have become interested in the Bideford, Westward Ho! & Appledore line – though it may be significant that the BET Company was undergoing a massive expansion at the turn of the century. Large and small tramways throughout Britain were falling into the BET net at this time, typical BET acquisitions during the period 1898–1902 being the Leamington & Warwick Tramway Company, the Kinver Light Railway, and Weston-super-Mare Tramways.

Some of the companies purchased or promoted by the British Electric Traction Company were ordinary urban street tramways, but several other BET companies were holiday or recreational lines in rural areas. The Kinver Light Railway, for example, was a sort of hybrid railway/tramway running from Stourbridge to a nearby beauty spot, and lines such as this had many affinities with the Bideford, Westward Ho! & Appledore route. If the Westward Ho! line could be extended along the picturesque North Devon

The scene on Bideford Quay as navvies dig up the roadway prior to laying the longitudinal timber baulks which will support the new railway. *Rob Dark Collection*

Construction under way near the Technical School; the longitudinal sleepers used on this part of the BWH&AR line can be clearly seen. Victoria Park can be glimpsed in the background. *Rob Dark Collection*

coast to Clovelly it would attract many summer tourists, and this potential for expansion may have been an additional factor in the BET company's desire to take control of the line from its original owners.

Whatever reasons may have prompted the BET takeover, the fact remains that control passed from local hands and into the hands of a large tramway company. This change of ownership was reflected in a number of Boardroom changes, notably the removal of most local Directors, leaving only Captain Molesworth to represent local interests on a Board which was dominated by British Electric Traction nominees.

The British Electric Traction Company was happy to see the Bideford, Westward Ho! & Appledore Railway remain in being as a distinct undertaking with its own devolved management and corporate identity, and to that extent the takeover was not necessarily a bad thing. Moreover, the BET Company was an energetic and expanding concern, and under BET auspices the Westward Ho! line was hurried to completion.

The Scheme Proceeds

The railway was soon more or less complete between Bideford Quay and Westward Ho!, and in the early months of 1900 the Board of Trade was officially notified that the line would soon be ready for its compulsory Board of Trade inspection.

Further progress was made in the following summer, and on 23rd August the *North Devon Journal* reported that 'the first new carriages' had been delivered across Bideford's historic bridge. These coaches, which had earlier been ordered from the Bristol Carriage & Wagon Works Company, were brought across the bridge in pieces, their heavy metal bogies being sent over first while the wooden bodies followed immediately afterwards. The new vehicles were re-assembled shortly afterwards, and Bideford people were intrigued to discover that these large bogie coaches were constructed on American lines, with open platforms at either end and a central gangway between two rows of tram-type seats.

Having acquired control of the Bideford, Westward Ho! & Appledore line the British Electric Traction Company started to take an interest in the railway, and Stephen Sellon, the BET's Chief Engineer, was soon in regular contact with the Board of Trade. The BET takeover had delayed earlier plans for a Board of Trade inspection, but on 15th March, 1901 Mr Sellon informed the BoT that the first portions of the Westward Ho! line were now ready for inspection.

The dispute with the local authorities had, in the intervening weeks and months, shown no sign of abating, but Mr Sellon seemed confident that the British Electric Traction Company would be able to resolve all points of difference in respect of 'Railway or Tramway Number One'. Displaying more than a hint of naivity, he told the Board of Trade that the original company had got into what he described as a 'hopeless muddle' over the quayside tramway – the implication being that the BET Company would never have allowed such problems to arise.

In reality, the Town Council was so determined to oppose the railway that it is unlikely that the British Electric Traction Company would have fared any better in the ongoing fight with the local burgesses. Moreover, matters were now in such a confused state that the problems simply could not be resolved overnight.

One especial difficulty had arisen prior to the BET takeover; in an attempt to reach a compromise with the local politicians, the railway company had (unwisely) agreed to shorten the length of Railway Number One. This was not in itself a problem, but in agreeing to reduce the length of trackwork on the Broad Quay the railway Directors had inadvertently led the Town Council to believed that only *one* line would be laid. This gave further ammunition to the local authorities, who were able to object to the provision of a run-round loop at the quayside terminus.

The BET Engineer evidently thought that when this matter was explained to the Board of Trade, the BoT would automatically take the side of the railway company. Unfortunately, the matter could not be so easily resolved, and although the line was ready for opening between Bideford Quay and Northam by the early months of 1901, it appeared that for legal reasons no run-round loop could be installed!

In the meantime, three small 2–4–2T locomotives which had been ordered from the Hunslet Engine Company by the original company had arrived in Bideford, and although the Westward Ho! line could not be opened for public traffic until it had passed its Board of Trade inspection, the BET authorities decided to stage a ceremonial 'opening' of the first five and a half miles of line between Bideford and Northam. It was agreed that the ceremonial opening would take place on 24th April, 1901, and as the Opening Day approached, local people began to look forward to a day of speeches and celebrations.

Opening of the Line

Opening Day was, as usual in such circumstances, treated as a public holiday in Bideford and the surrounding area. The dispute with the Town Council was temporarily laid aside, and, on a sunny spring day, some 200 invited guests assembled at Curtis's Marsh, from where a special train would take them on an inaugural trip to Westward Ho!. With 'Herr Groop's German Band' in attendance, a large and enthusiastic crowd watched in admiration as the 2–4–2T locomotive *Grenville* prepared to depart with a two coach train.

The day's events were described shortly afterwards in *The Bideford Gazette*, and under the headlines 'To Westward Ho! by Rail' and 'A Pleasant Ride and Social Function', the paper reported the great occasion as follows:

> Punctual to time, an engine decked with a Union Jack pushed two of the company's handsome carriages into position, and soon all who had accepted the kind invitation were seated. With a shrill whistle, and a locomotive snort, the train started off at a pace which would put to shame some of the big trunk line trains.

'The cheers of those assembled to see the company off', continued the reporter, 'had scarcely died away, when the chorus was taken up by ... groups along the line at the various level crossings'. Continuing in similar vein, the writer expressed his delight at the charming scenery that unfolded as the two coach special proceeded in triumph along the sylvan Kenwith Valley.

Passing the crossing station at Abbotsham Road, the 'First train' ascended towards the spectacular coastal section along Cornborough Cliffs, after which the special ran downhill towards Westward Ho!. Here, the inaugural train came to a stand at the site of the unfinished station near Nelson Terrace, and after receiving the congratulations of those who had gathered to participate in the opening ceremonies the invited guests were taken on to the end of the line at Northam. Herr Groop's bandsmen travelled aboard the train and played appropriate music en route, and the day's festivities included a break for tea and other refreshments at Westward Ho!.

In addition to describing the Opening Day celebrations in considerable detail *The Bideford Gazette* also printed an interesting description of the railway as it appeared at the very start of its life, and some of this useful information is worth repeating. The following extract contains details of the newly-completed line from Bideford to Westward Ho! and Northam, together with a summary of the fares and train services that were expected to be provided on the Westward Ho! line:

> When the railway is opened – which it is expected to be on an early day – trains will run about every three quarters of an hour, starting from Bideford at 8 am.
>
> The third class fare for the single journey will be 5d. between Bideford and Westward Ho! while first class passengers will pay 8d. for the single, or 1s. for the return journey. On Mondays, Wednesdays and Fridays it is intended to run excursions at 6d. return. Bathing trains will be run in the season, and will form a feature of the Sunday traffic.
>
> The opening of the line is the consummation of an idea long cherished. In 1872, the late Earl of Iddesleigh, then Sir Stafford Northcote, cut the first sod of a line which was intended to serve the district now about to be opened up. But the hopes of the early promoters were disappointed. Difficulties arose, and the scheme was dropped. A few years ago it was revived chiefly through the instrumentality of Captain Molesworth RN, and Mr Taylor, who are large owners of land in the neighbourhood, and whose interest in it was stimulated by the remarkable development of Westward Ho!.

The paper explained that 'Mr J.T. Jervis, CE, the main engineer of the line to connect north and south Devon by way of Torrington and Okehampton was engaged upon the scheme', and plans were then made for the construction of a three feet gauge line to Westward Ho!. Afterwards, added the *Gazette*, the scheme was modified, and the line was eventually built as a 4 ft 8½ in. gauge route:

> It is single throughout its length of five and a half miles, and though differing but little from an ordinary railway has in the details of its construction one or two interesting features. Starting from Bideford Quay, it is for about a quarter of a mile constructed on the tramway principle. At this spot the space between the lines, and a foot or two on either side, is paved with Jarrah wood blocks at the level of the ordinary roadway.
>
> Leaving the Quay the line traverses the reclaimed Pill and then becomes an ordinary railway laid on tranverse sleepers. Although there are several steam tramways, it is a novelty to see railway engines and trains traversing public streets in this country; and this portion of the scheme has been viewed with misgivings by some of the people of Bideford.

The inaugural train poses for the camera during the Opening Day celebrations held on 24th April, 1901; Herr Group's 'German' bandsmen can be seen in the foreground.
Rob Dark Collection

The Opening Day special pauses in the unfinished station at Westward Ho! This view clearly shows the extreme width of the BWH&AR coaches, which (as originally constructed) were no less than 11 ft 3 in. wide across the steps at each end.
Rob Dark Collection

Considerable controversy has taken place between the Corporation and the Company as to the manner in which this part of the undertaking should be carried out. The Company wanted a loop line on the Quay in order to reverse the engines, but they were unable to come to terms with the Corporation and the line is now being completed as a single line. In working the traffic it will, therefore, be necessary to keep a spare engine and run this down to the rear of the train to make a fresh start on each journey. As there are to be two trains and three engines, there will always be an engine in reserve, and each of them will in turn draw the train to Northam.

Having alluded to the simmering dispute between the railway company and the local authorities, *The Bideford Gazette* report described the route of the line between Bideford and Northam:

After leaving the Pill the line is continued on a rising gradient to Abbotsham Cliffs, from which magnificent views of the coast line from Baggy Point to Clovelly and Hartland Point are obtainable. Here a crossing place has been constructed and the trains will stop to put down and pick up passengers.

Following the contour of the cliffs the line quickly runs down to Westward Ho! where there is another station close to the United Services College and several of the hotels. A mile or so beyond is the present terminus adjacent to the road from Northam to Pimpley and near to the Golf Links.

In the scheme as sanctioned by Parliament powers were given to make the line to Appledore, and its full title is The Bideford, Westward Ho! & Appledore Railway. But for the present it is not intended to continue the line to Appledore.

The carriages are built on the American principle with a central corridor and are entered like tramcars from the ends instead of the sides. They are roomy, comfortably seated, well ventilated and abundantly lighted. Each coach measures 40 ft in length and has a width of 9 ft. They will seat ten first class and forty third class passengers. Two coaches will make up a train.

As the tickets will be issued by the conductors of the trains there are no ticket offices. Mr W.J. Gale is the Resident Engineer and Mr Henry Sowden the Traffic Superintendent.

The ceremonial 'opening' of the line was an immense success in terms of public relations and advanced publicity, but there was still much to be done before the line could commence regular operation. The Board of Trade inspection had not yet taken place, but on 14th May, 1901 Colonel H.A. Yorke of the BoT traversed the railway on his inspection tour. Unfortunately, the Inspector was not entirely pleased with the new line, and he refused to 'pass' the quayside tramway for public traffic. Colonel Yorke also found fault with the engine, though he was generally satisfied with the railway section between the Pill at Bideford and Northam.

Amusingly, the Inspector had been accosted by a group of angry residents from the Chanter's Lane and Causeway areas, who claimed that the level crossings installed at those places were dangerous. The Causeway level crossing had, in fact, caused considerable local disquiet because the main road from Bideford to Northam passed over the railway at that point. The protesters (some of whom may have been genuinely worried about the risk of road accidents) claimed that a bridge should have been erected, and for this reason Colonel Yorke devoted much attention to the arrangements for working the gates and signalling the line at the Causeway.

The Board of Trade Inspection Report

Having carefully examined the railway from end to end, Colonel Yorke prepared a copious inspection report that filled several typed pages.[13] This document, dated 18th May, 1901, is worth quoting in detail insofar as it provides very full details of the track, signalling, stations and engineering features of the Bideford, Westward Ho! & Appledore line.

As usual, the BoT Inspector commenced his report with an elegant introduction, and then immediately launched into a detailed technical description:

18th May, 1901

Sir,
I have the honour to report, for the information of the Board of Trade, that in accordance with the instructions contained in your minute of the 1st May, I inspected on the 14th *inst* the Bideford, Westward Ho! & Appledore Railway.
This is a composite undertaking, partly railway, partly tramway, and possessing some unusual features, which has been constructed under the Bideford, Westward Ho! & Appledore Act of 1896.

With meticulous accuracy, Colonel Yorke then explained that Railway or Tramway Number One on Bideford Quay was a tramway, whereas Railway Number Two was (apart from a short length of tramway at its eastern end) a conventional railway with sleepered track; Railway Number Three, from Westward Ho! to Appledore, was also a railway, but only a small portion of that line had been constructed.

After making this important distinction between the railway and tramway sections of the Westward Ho! line, Colonel Yorke turned his attention to the railway between Bideford and Northam:

The permanent way is laid with flat-bottomed steel rails weighing 60 lb per yard, which are attached to sleepers (9 ft × 9 inches × 4½ inches) by fang bolts and clips, and dog spikes, in the manner shown on the drawing supplied by the Company.
The ballast is of broken stone, and is said to be laid to a depth of twelve inches below the sleepers. The 'road' is in very good condition.
The steepest gradient has an inclination of 1 in 40, and the sharpest curve a radius of 5 chains. This curve only extends for a length of 1.74 chains, and is at the junction of the railway and the tramway. It is, in accordance with the Parliamentary plans, fitted with a check rail . . . The fencing of the line, which consists of either post and rail or wire, is sufficient, except at the places where the banks between the fields adjacent to the line abut on to the fences, at which points the height of the fences should be increased.
The stations on the railway are Westward Ho! and Northam. At the former there are two platforms, each 320 ft long and one foot above rail level. Waiting rooms and conveniences for both sexes are being built on the up platform, but these are not altogether complete.
At Northam, which is at the end of the line as at present constructed, there is a single platform, 180 ft long and 6 inches high, on which is erected a small shed. At this terminal station the shed does not appear to afford sufficient accommodation, and the Company should provide a larger waiting room and a convenience for men. Booking offices are nowhere necessary, as tickets will be issued on the trains by the conductors.

Name boards are required at the stations, and, if the line is to be used after dark, lamps should be provided.

The height of the platforms, though far below the standard requirements of the Board of Trade, is sufficient, as the carriages to be used on the line have no side doors, but have end gangways and steps, the lowest being 12 inches from the ground.

Clocks need not be placed in the stations, but should be provided in the signal boxes.

The BoT Inspector explained that the Company was 'desirous of making small platforms about 20 ft × 30 ft long' at Chanter's Lane, Causeway Crossing, Mudcott passing loop, and at one or two other places where public roads crossed the line in convenient proximity to nearby houses or farms. These platforms would be six inches above rail level, and fenced at the back, but there would be no shelters for waiting travellers. Colonel Yorke had no objections to the provision of such platforms, but he warned that name boards would be required, and if the halts were to be used at night some form of lighting would be necessary.

The next part of the BoT report dealt with cuttings and other earthworks on the newly-constructed line, after which Colonel Yorke described the bridges and culverts that had been provided *en route* to Northam:

> The deepest cutting has a depth of 32 ft, and the highest embankment a height of 32 ft. The geological formation is mostly rock, shale or shillet, and the side slopes of both cuttings and embankments are standing well.
>
> There are two bridges under the line, one with a span of 10 ft and the other of 12 ft. Both are constructed of steel troughs resting on masonry abutments. There are also five culverts constructed in the same manner, and with the same materials as the bridges. These works are standing well; the steel troughs have sufficient theoretical strength, and showed hardly any deflection when tested.

Three of the level crossings on the line were protected by semaphore signals, the crossings in question being at Chanter's Lane, the Causeway and Mudcott passing loop. In view of the objections that had been raised locally in respect of the Causeway level crossing the Colonel had evidently considered whether a bridge would be more suitable at this busy location. However, he decided that a bridge would 'be a very costly undertaking', and although the Inspector agreed with some of the objections that had been made, he felt that the situation would be improved if a raised signal box and better signalling could be installed.

As originally constructed, the gates at the Causeway were worked by a resident gateman and protected by up and down 'stop' signals on a common post.[14] These arrangements were clearly inadequate at a busy level crossing, and instead the Inspector demanded that proper signals should be installed on each side of the gates.

In stipulating a 'raised signal box', he ordered that the cabin should be 'so placed as to afford a good view along the road and along the railway', and, furthermore, the box would need a proper 'gate wheel and other reliable mechanism for enabling the gateman to open and close the gates simultaneously and rapidly'.

Still dealing with signalling matters, the report listed the various signal boxes on the line from Bideford to Northam. There were, in fact, four signal cabins on the Westward Ho! line at the time of its BoT inspection, the largest of which, as Bideford Yard, had 11 working levers and three spares. The box at Westward Ho! station had four working levers and four spares, while at Northam the signal cabin had four levers in use and one spare; the fourth box, at Mudcott passing loop, originally had five working levers and three spares.

In general, there were no real problems on the railway section between Bideford and Northam, and Colonel Yorke was able to 'pass' this part of the BWH&AR line for public opening subject to the usual BoT requirements in respect of single line operation, and on condition that the various deficiencies mentioned in the report were rectified prior to re-inspection by a Board of Trade Inspector.

The second half of Colonel Yorke's voluminous inspection report dealt with the tramway section along Bideford Quay, and here the Colonel identified a number of deficiencies – all of which would have to be rectified before 'Railway or Tramway Number One' could be opened for public traffic.

The most serious problem concerned the grooves in the recessed line along the roadway; these were far too wide, and the Inspector considered that they constituted a very real danger to road users.

The three BWH&AR engines were perfectly adequate for use on the railway section, but they required modification before they could be safely employed on the tramway. Proper 'fenders', for example, were needed in order to prevent horses or pedestrians from falling under the wheels, while there should, strictly speaking, have been a seat for the driver at the front of each locomotive.

Colonel Yorke was displeased with the lack of 'fenders' (cow catchers) on the engines, but with a commendable degree of common sense he realised that the requirement for a 'seat for the driver' applied to self-contained tramcars rather than railway locomotives; for this reason he considered that the objection would be overcome if the fireman stood at the front of the engines as they slowly passed along the street section at a prescribed speed of no more than 4 mph.

The large bogie coaches ordered by the BWH&AR were ideally-suited for use on the railway, but the BoT Inspector noted that, with a maximum width of 11 ft 3 in. they projected too far on each side of the tram lines. This problem would, he thought, be solved if the steps at each end of the cars were modified.

Another potential danger identified during the Board of Trade inspection concerned the mechanism for operation of a siding that had been laid along the very edge of the quay. Colonel Yorke was horrified to discover that the siding points were worked from an open lever that could – conceivably – be tampered with by members of the public. Such open lever frames were quite safe within the fenced-off confines of a conventional goods yard or station, but they were unacceptable on a street tramway, and the Inspector ordered that the offending points should, in future, be worked with the aid of a detachable lever which would only be inserted into the mechanism when the siding was in use.

In view of all these deficiencies, the Board of Trade Inspector was unable to 'pass' the quayside tramway for public traffic, but as the major part of the line to Northam and Westward Ho! had been officially passed as safe for the conveyance of passengers, the Bideford, Westward Ho! & Appledore Railway was opened for public traffic on Monday 20th May, 1901.[15]

Some Further Details of the Line

The newly-opened railway was a single track route with intermediate passing loops at Bideford Yard (½ mile), Mudcott (2½ miles), and Westward Ho! (4¾ miles). At Northam, the railway terminated in a single platform station beside a short run-round loop.

Stations or other stopping places were originally provided at Bideford Yard, Mudcott, Westward Ho! and Northam, while the additional halts referred to by Colonel Yorke were brought into use at, or shortly after, the public opening of the line on 20th May, 1901; these halts were situated at Strand Road, Chanter's Lane, The Causeway, Kenwith Castle, Cornborough Cliffs and Beach Road.

The tramway terminus on Bideford Quay was (apparently) brought into use as soon as the problems mentioned in Colonel Yorke's inspection report had been remedied – although, as we shall see, this short section of the BWH&AR line continued to generate local controversy long after the opening of the railway.

The single line was worked on the train-staff-and-ticket system whereby an up or down series of trains were allowed to follow each other into a staff section after their drivers had been issued with small 'tickets' that permitted them to proceed;[16] the actual train staff would then be taken to the end of the section on the last train of an up or down series. This system was more flexible than the standard train staff method of single line operation, and the BWH&AR management clearly hoped that large numbers of special excursion trains would run to and from Westward Ho! during the summer holiday period.

The train staff sections at the time of opening were Bideford Yard to Mudcott, Mudcott to Westward Ho! and Westward Ho! to Northam. An additional staff section from Bideford Quay to Bideford Yard was introduced when the tramway section was opened for traffic. (Mudcott passing loop was renamed 'Abbotsham Road' when the passenger platforms at that point were brought into public use.)

The new railway was worked by the three Hunslet 2–4–2Ts that had been delivered shortly before the ceremonial opening, and there were, for the first few months, just four passenger vehicles.

Two-coach trains were the norm, though as some of the new bogie coaches lacked guards' compartments an ordinary four-wheeled brake van was sometimes marshalled in formation with the passenger vehicles.[17] There were also eight goods wagons, and these were used for both engineering work and freight traffic between Bideford Quay and Westward Ho! gas works – a short siding being provided at the latter place for coal traffic.

Holiday traffic was an important element in Bideford, Westward Ho! & Appledore operations, and with the aim of fostering the railway's image as a tourist line running through historic Devon towns and villages, the three engines were given names reflecting local history and traditions. Perhaps inevitably, one of the three 2–4–2Ts was named *Grenville* in honour of Bideford's greatest local hero, while the two remaining engines were named *Torridge* and *Kingsley* respectively.

A two coach train ventures to the very end of the line at Bideford Quay, as seen on a heavily retouched postcard. *Oakwood Collection*

Engineering work under way on Bideford Quay. This turn-of-the-century view shows work taking place around the quayside siding – probably in connection with the changes ordered by the Board of Trade Inspector. *Rob Dark Collection*

Further work takes place on Bideford Quay, as gangs of navvies lay the controversial loop line alongside the main running line. Note the BWH&AR open wagons, which were used for engineering duties and occasional freight traffic. *Rob Dark Collection*

Chapter Three
Extension to Appledore

The Westward Ho! line was opened at the start of the 1901 holiday season, and this ensured that receipts, for the next few weeks at least, were particularly good. On 30th May, 1901 *The North Devon Journal* suggested that Pebble Ridge and the nearby beach at Westward Ho! was becoming as busy as Weston-super-Mare; the railway was said to be carrying a 'very heavy' summer traffic, and the paper wondered if the railway company would have to obtain additional rolling stock 'in order to accommodate the crowds' who were 'so anxious to travel by their line'.

The railway was worked intensively, with trains running at approximately 40 minute intervals during the height of the summer. Many tourists were conveyed over the line, while local people were also very eager to travel over the new route to Westward Ho!. There was, inevitably, an air of novelty about the newly-opened line during these first weeks of operation, and the railway's supporters must have been gratified by the sight of ordinary Bideford people enjoying their first rides on the line! Indeed, on the evidence of local newspaper reports, it appears that public response to the Westward Ho! line was generally favourable.

Abandonment of the Clovelly Scheme

There was, at this time, apparent indecision in regard to the authorised line to Clovelly and the extension to Appledore. The British Electric Traction Company was, it appeared, interested in extending the line in a westerly direction towards Clovelly and Hartland, but the BET Company intended that this Hartland extension would be built and operated by 'The Western Counties Electric Railways & Tramway Company' rather than by the moribund Bideford & Clovelly Railway.

The Western Counties company, which had been founded in 1897, was a tramway undertaking rather than a railway, and perhaps for this reason the BET management decided that the Bideford to Hartland route would be worked as an electrified system; with talk of the Bideford, Westward Ho! & Appledore line being adapted for electric operation the Bideford & Clovelly scheme was quietly dropped, and the scheme was formally abandoned in 1901.[18]

The future of the Appledore extension also seemed to be in some doubt – though it is possible that the BET company was waiting to see how much traffic was generated by the Westward Ho! line before proceeding with construction of the 1½ mile extension to Appledore.

Although trains were now running to Bideford Quay the lack of a run-round loop was a major problem. A spare engine had to be kept in readiness at Bideford Yard to deal with incoming trains, and this meant that the company's wage and fuel bills were much higher than they would otherwise have been. The problem was particularly acute during the winter months, when the BWH&AR was obliged to use two engines to work the much-reduced off-season service. As far as the railway company was concerned the situation was intolerable, and it was clear that, sooner or later, a major row would erupt between the railway and the Borough Council.

Renewed Problems at Bideford

The long-standing dispute with Bideford Town Council degenerated into open conflict in the early months of 1902, this deterioration being caused (ostensibly) by the railway company which, having struggled for several months to operate the line without a run-round loop at its southern terminus, decided to take unilateral action. Assuming that Parliament had always intended a loop line to be provided, the railway authorities started digging up the roadway along Bideford Quay in order that a second line of rails could be laid.

The Town Council was furious – although the railway could legitimately point to the 1896 Act of Parliament, which had stipulated that three chains of 'Railway or Tramway Number One', would be 'double line'. The British Electric Traction Company's view was, quite simply, that the railway was 'carrying out the construction of the tramway in accordance with the provisions of the Bideford, Westward Ho! & Appledore Railway Act of 21st May, 1896'.

The railway company may also have assumed that, with or without a run-round loop, relations with the Borough Council could hardly have been worse. The local authorities had already taken the railway to court on the pretext that, on 18th May, 1901, a train had ventured onto the quay without council permission. The case was brought before Bideford Petty Sessions in July 1901, and the proceedings were reported in the pages of *The Railway Times* on 20th July, 1901; the paper described the case as follows:

> BIDEFORD, WESTWARD HO! & APPLEDORE RAILWAY – The Bideford, Westward Ho! & Appledore Railway Company were, at Bideford on Monday, summoned at the instance of the Town Council for having, on the 18th May last, used the line over Bideford Quay, which was not in accordance with . . . their special Act of Parliament.
>
> Mr W.B. Seldon, Town Clerk, said there were five summonses in all. One was for running the engine over Bideford Quay without having previously come to an agreement with the Council as to the use and maintenance of the line thereon, as required by Section Fifty Eight of the special Act of Parliament of the Bideford, Westward Ho! & Appledore Railway, and the other four dealt with special appliances required under the Act to be fitted to the engines, there being a summons for each as follows: A speed indicator, a special bell or whistle, a fender to push away obstructions and a seat for the driver in front of the engine.
>
> As a result of correspondence having taken place, the railway company had consented to a conviction of ten shillings inclusive in each case.
>
> For the Corporation, he would say that the proceedings were not taken with any idea of harassing the Company in any proper and legitimate use of the railway on the quay as provided for by the special Act of Parliament, but mainly for the safeguarding of the public.
>
> A fine was then inflicted in each case. It was mentioned that the Company had also agreed to pay £10 10s. towards the costs of the Corporation in the matter.

In retrospect, this first legal tussle between Bideford Borough Council and the Bideford, Westward Ho! & Appledore Railway exhibited many elements of farce. The quayside tramway had, only four days previously, failed its compulsory Board of Trade inspection, and the railway company had clearly had no intention of running *public* trains on the quay on 18th May, 1901. Furthermore, the Board of Trade Inspector had himself criticised the railway for failing to equip the BWH&AR engines with the 'special appliances' that had been mentioned by the Council.

Without Board of Trade approval the raiway company could never have opened the quayside line for public traffic, and there were thus no grounds whatsoever for the Corporation to claim that the quayside tramway was being operated by a poorly-equipped engine without fenders, bells or other necessary equipment. On top of all this the Town Clerk had felt compelled to add that the Corporation was not 'harassing' the railway, and that the local authority was only interested in 'the safeguarding of the public'; these somewhat hypocritical claims can have done little to ease the tension that existed between the railway and the local authorities.

The 1901 court case seems to have been brought mainly because the railway had not consulted the council prior to starting work required as a result of the BoT inspection, and as that urgent remedial work had inevitably involved use of the quayside tramway, the local authorities were able to take the railway to court. The court in question was, moreover, the local magistrate's court – and there was little chance of the railway company getting a fair hearing before magistrates who, in all probability, were personal friends of those same councillors who had persistently opposed the building of a railway along Bideford's picturesque Broad Quay.

The local authorities, in fact, wished that the railway had not been laid on the quay in the first place, and in this context some local politicians argued that the reclaimed 'Pill' to the north of the Technical School would have made a much more convenient site for a railway terminus. Others suggested that the tramway section of Railway Number One could easily have been diverted to run nearer to the river, and away from the public roadway. Sadly, the railway company rejected both of these suggestions, and both parties having failed to reach any kind of compromise, the Town Council applied for an injunction to force the BWH&AR to remove the offending second line.

The Bideford, Westward Ho! & Appledore line was an unimportant provincial railway, but its continuing dispute with the local authorities gained it a modicum of national publicity which would not otherwise have been obtained. Specialist railway journals such as *The Railway Times* reported that legal proceedings had been commenced – although, perversely, the latter journal seems to have sided with the Town Council against the railway. One might, perhaps, have expected a railway-orientated periodical to understand the need for a loop line for running-round purposes, but on 13th September, 1902 *The Railway Times* printed the following pro-council report:

> The long standing dispute between Bideford Town Council and the company which owns the railway to Westward Ho! has at last reached a climax.
> The keen desire of the Company to obtain a loop line at the starting point at Bideford has been referred to on previous occasions in connection with the suggestion that a compromise, which would have the effect of freeing the thoroughfare by the river from railway lines, might be effected. Instead of peace, however, there is war; so far from a compromise being arranged, litigation is

imminent. The Company are the aggressors. Their high handed action in making the loop line in the face of the decided refusal of the council to permit such a thing and the recent intimation of the Board of Trade that either the consent of the local authority or an Act of Parliament was necessary has forced a fight, and the challenge boldly given has been taken up eagerly.

Bideford folk are in high dudgeon at what their chief magistrate characterised as 'impudent outrage' and 'illegal encroachment'. Their indignation has found vent in the commencement of proceedings for an injunction by the council, and in a decided protest of the ratepayers.

The burgesses are united against the granting of any concession, and confident that in this brush the Company have overstepped the legal mark and will have to retire. In view of the decision of the Board of Trade but a few months earlier, there seems to be a deal in their contention.

Now that the parties have again come into direct collision it is to be hoped that the outstanding differences will be settled once and for all, so that in the future the interests of the town and of the railway will be mutual.

The case was heard before Mr Justice Swinten Eady in the closing months of 1902, and on 13th December, 1902 *The Railway Times* reported that the action was proceeding. Eventually, the Borough Council managed to obtain their injunction, and the railway company was ordered to pull up the offending rails.

The Light Railway Order of 1904

This was not, however, the end of the affair and the BWH&AR was far from beaten. In a new attempt to break the deadlock, it was suggested (possibly by Stephen Sellon or some other BET Company official) that the Bideford, Westward Ho! & Appledore Railway should apply for new Powers giving specific authority for additional lines on the Broad Quay at Bideford. As the original Powers for construction of the line to Appledore had lapsed five years after the passing of the 1896 Act, the BET Company also needed renewed authorisation for the extension line from Northam to Appledore, and it was agreed that a Light Railway Order should be obtained, giving authority for both the loop line *and* the Appledore extension.

As we have seen, the original portions of the Bideford, Westward Ho! & Appledore line had been constructed under the provisions of an Act of Parliament, but as the Light Railways Act of 1896 was now on the statute books, a further Act of Parliament was deemed unnecessary. The British Electric Traction Company was familiar with the procedures established under the Light Railways Act, and the company had already obtained numerous Light Railway Orders in connection with its other subsidiary lines. Accordingly, an application was made to the Light Railway Commissioners, and the Commissioners having responded favourably, the necessary Light Railway Order was made in 1904.

The Order itself was a complex document providing consent for a series of new lines which, for convenience, were listed in numerical sequence.[19] The most important of these new lines were designated 'Railway Number One' and 'Railway Number Three', Railway Number One being the Appledore extension while Railway Number Three was the much-needed run-round loop on Bideford Quay.

Confusingly, the numbering sequence employed in the Light Railway Order of 1904 did not correspond to the sequence that had been used in the Bideford, Westward Ho! & Appledore Act of 1896, and for this reason the Railway Number Three of 1896 became Railway Number One in the 1904 Order.

There was, to some extent, a certain logic in the changed numbering system because part of the 1896 Railway Number Three had in fact been built – the line in question being the section of BWH&AR route between Westward Ho! and Northam. In effect, the new Railway Number One would start from the end of the original Railway Number Three, and this point was clearly made in the Light Railway Order, which defined Railway Number One as a railway:

> 1 mile 3 furlongs 9.50 chains in thereabouts in length wholly situate in the Parish of Northam in the County of Devon, commencing by a junction with the Parliamentary Railway and its termination at Northam Station, proceeding thence in a north-easterly direction and terminating near the western end of the Schools, Appledore.

It would be superfluous to examine the LRO description of Railway Number Three in detail because this short line was merely the run-round loop needed on Bideford Quay. It is worth noting, however, that various other short lines were authorised in the Light Railway Order, and these additional lines served as useful ammunition for the BWH&AR in its continuing battle with Bideford Town Council; the railway company now had Powers to build, not only the loop line, but also certain other lines in the Borough of Bideford, and as the Light Railway Commissioners had agreed that these lines were necessary the local authorities could do very little to prevent the company from carrying out its latest plans.

Armed with its new Powers in respect of the loop line on Bideford Quay, the railway company was able to reinstate the additional rails beside the existing running line in the centre of the roadway; these new rails were laid on longitudinal timber sleepers which were, in turn, buried in the road surface and paved with wooden blocks. In theory, the smooth surface so created enabled road users to use the quay as a normal road, though there were, in fact, numerous complaints about the slippery nature of the wooden blocks. (Oil from the engines was a particular problem in wet weather.)

In addition to re-laying the loop line on Bideford Quay, the railway authorities decided that significant economies could be made if some of the less important level crossings on the line between Causeway Crossing and Northam could be made into 'open' crossings protected only by cattle guards.

It was, in theory at least, a comparatively simple matter to take down level crossing gates and install cattle guards in their place, but anti-railway feeling was running so high at this time that local residents (some of whom had earlier complained about the Causeway Crossing) decided to make the matter of cattle guards versus crossing gates into a major issue. As on previous occasions, the Board of Trade was bombarded with letters and protests about the railway, the implication being that cattle guards were intrinsically unsafe.

Plans of the proposed cattle guards were examined in great detail in an attempt to prove that the idea was unsound, and the Board of Trade was again drawn into the conflict as an arbiter between the railway, the local authorities and the protesting ratepayers. In December 1904 Major J.W. Pringle of the Board of Trade visited the level crossings which the Company intended to turn into open crossings, and to the chagrin of the local protesters he approved the plan in principle, subject to final inspection of the completed cattle guards.

Colonel Yorke's Re-inspection

A few months previously, in March 1903, Colonel H.A. Yorke had again inspected the Bideford, Westward Ho! & Appledore line to ensure that the various changes required at the time of his initial inspection had been put into effect.[20] On this occasion, the Inspector could find little to complain about and, having satisfied himself that the 'raised signal box', altered fencing and other requirements had been properly carried out, he wrote the following brief report:

26th March, 1903

Sir,
I have the honour to report, for the information of the Board of Trade, that in compliance with the instructions contained in your minute of the 26th March, 1902 and 21st November, 1902, I have re-inspected the Bideford, Westward Ho! & Appledore Light Railway as far as Railway Number Two and Tramway Number One are concerned.
As regards Railway Number Two, I found that all the requirements in my report dated 18th May, 1901 have been satisfactorily complied with.

I have the honour, etc.,
H.A. Yorke, Lt-Colonel, RE.

Colonel Yorke's oblique reference to Tramway Number One is slightly confusing in the sense that he appears to have refrained from passing judgement on this section of the Bideford, Westward Ho! & Appledore line. This may be because, at the time of the inspection, the outcome of the dispute between the railway and the town council had not been resolved, and if the case was still *sub judice* the Colonel would have been understandably reluctant to cloud the issue by making any kind of pronouncement in respect of the loop line.

Final Inspection of the Bideford Loop Line

In retrospect, it made little difference whether Colonel Yorke inspected that quayside lines or not because, having decided to obtain new Powers under the LRO the Bideford, Westward Ho! & Appledore Railway was able to transform the entire legal situation. The loop line authorised as Railway Number Three in the Light Railway Order was in place by the end of 1904, and on 17th December, 1904 Major Pringle was able to carry out an inspection of the new works at the time of his visit to the level crossings.

Major Pringle could find nothing amiss with the run-round loop, and he immediately 'passed' the new line for public traffic. His inspection report,[21]

A BWH&AR coach and two of the company's three 2–4–2T locomotives attract much attention on Bideford Quay. The steps (and seats) attached to the leading engine suggest that the photographs may have been taken during Colonel Yorke's 1901 BoT inspection trip. *Rob Dark Collection*

One of the Bideford, Westward Ho! & Appledore Railway's coaches is re-united with its bogies after delivery to the BWH&AR line. *Rob Dark Collection*

dated 17th December, 1904, is simple and straightforward, but in view of the long and complex struggle that had been waged by the railway in order to build this short line, it would be appropriate to print this final report in full:

17th December, 1904

Sir,

I have the honour to report, for the information of the Board of Trade, that in compliance with the instructions contained in your minute of the 5th instant I made an inspection today of the new works on the Bideford, Westward Ho! & Appledore Railway.

A loop line, about 110 yards in length has been laid on the Broad Quay at Bideford. This forms Railway Number Three authorised by the Light Railway Order of 1904.

The loop is to be used for passenger traffic, and to enable engines to run-round their trains. The loop points are worked by hand. The permanent way is in a satisfactory condition.

Subject to a speed limit of 4 miles per hour on the loop I can recommend the Board to authorise the new light railway for passenger traffic.

I have the honour, etc.,
J.W. Pringle, Major

After a sustained struggle lasting for no less than seven years, the railway had finally managed to secure its run-round loop, but this important victory over the forces of local reaction was not, by any means, the end of the war. There were still people who, obsessed with hatred towards the Bideford, Westward Ho! & Appledore Railway and all its works, wished to turn the cattle guards dispute into something approaching a major issue. Letters continued to wing their way between Bideford and the Board of Trade in London, the precise design, construction, and even the *colour* of the proposed cattle guards being the subject of much dispute.

On 22nd February, 1905, Major Pringle returned to Bideford in order to see the level crossings at Kenwith Road, Puse Hill, Abbotsham Road, Gas Works Lane and Hanger's Lane (the last-mentioned crossings being at Westward Ho!). Again, the Major expressed his approval of the proposed change from gated to ungated crossings at these places, and it was agreed that the gates could be taken down.

The work of conversion was put in hand in the following months, and on 31st August, 1905 Major Pringle paid another visit to the Bideford, Westward Ho! & Appledore line in order to carry out a formal inspection on behalf of the Board of Trade.

The gates had, he found, been taken away, and in their place the railway company had installed cattle guards constructed according to plans that had previously been agreed by the BoT. The new arrangements were, in Major Pringle's view, entirely satisfactory; the crossings had been properly protected with fixed speed and caution boards for both rail and road traffic, and the Board of Trade Inspector had no hesitation in approving the new gateless crossings on the Bideford, Westward Ho! & Appledore Railway.

In addition to installing the loop line on Bideford Quay and converting most of its level crossings to 'open' status, the railway had attempted to stimulate summer holiday traffic by building a 'Reception Hall for Concerts, Dances and Other Entertainments' beside the station at Westward Ho!. Here, throughout the summer season 'High Class Entertainments' were arranged for the delectation of the public, and combined rail and admission tickets were issued by the railway. Known as 'Station Hall', this new attraction was opened in 1903, and in accordance with BET Company practice, 'negro' minstrels and other entertainers were hired each summer by the railway company.

Completion of the Scheme

The years from 1905 until 1908 were a time of modest progress for the Bideford, Westward Ho! & Appledore Railway, and although it was never a spectacular success in the financial sense, summer loadings suggested that the line was viable as a holiday route. In these circumstances the line's owners decided that the BWH&AR should be completed throughout to Appledore, and with talk of electrification still in the air, the British Electric Traction Company started work on the final part of the route between Northam and the proposed terminus near the school house at Appledore.

The authorised route from Northam to Appledore presented few engineering difficulties, the terrain around Northam being relatively flat and featureless. Approaching Appledore, the chosen route skirted the coastline, while in Appledore itself the terminus of the line from Bideford and Westward Ho! would be situated on the north side of the little town, in an elevated position above Irsha Street.

Construction was well advanced by the closing months of 1907, the work being carried out under the supervision of Henry Sowden, the BWH&AR General Manager. In an attempt to keep construction costs to the barest minimum, the extension line was laid with second-hand rail, much of which was former main line 80 lb. per yard double-headed rail. Some domestic property was demolished to provide sufficient space for the terminal station at Appledore, but otherwise the 1 mile 39 chain extension from Northam was laid across mainly undeveloped land.

The work proceeded without major incident, although there was a brief moment of excitement in December 1907 when workmen digging near the station site at Appledore unearthed a long-buried human skull!

The extension line was ready for its complulsory Board of Trade inspection by the spring of 1908, and on 23rd April, 1908 Major J.W. Pringle returned once more to the BWH&AR line. As usual, the BoT Inspector produced a very full report,[22] with useful and interesting information about the recently-completed extension line. Some of this information is given below:

24th April, 1908

Sir,
I have the honour to report, for the information of the Board of Trade, that in compliance with the instructions contained in your minute of the 11th instant, I made an inspection yesterday of Light Railway Number One of the Bideford, Westward Ho! & Appledore Railway.
The railway is an extension of the existing railway which, commencing at Bideford, formerly terminated at Northam Station. The extension commences by an end-on junction at Northam Station and, running in a north-easterly direction, terminates at Appledore.

The total length of this new railway is 1 mile 39.65 chains. It is laid as a single line except at the terminus, and lies, I understand, within the authorised limit of deviation. The gauge is 4 ft 8½ inches.

Turning, first of all, to details of the trackwork and engineering, Major Pringle reported that the sharpest curve on the extension was of six chains radius. There were, he noted, several reverse curves without intervening sections of straight line, and the engineering was of typical light railway character:

> The earthwork is light in character, and nowhere exceeds seven feet in depth of cuttings or height of banks. The only bridge is for the use of foot passengers, across the line near the terminus. This bridge is approached on one side by a stair, and I observed that no midway landing had been provided, although the height of the bridge exceeds ten feet. But in the case of a light railway where crowding is unlikely this particular requirement may, I think, be waived.
>
> There are no tunnels, viaducts or culverts of five feet or more. The railway is fenced with galvanised wires, four feet in height.

The level crossings, continued Major Pringle, were equipped with cattle guards to prevent cows or other animals from straying onto the line. As far as permanent way was concerned, the extension was formed of rails which were:

> Chiefly double headed second hand rail, formerly weighing 80 lb. per yard. These rest in cast iron chairs, 40 lb. in weight, which are secured to second hand sleepers, 9 ft × 10 inches × 5 inches. Broken stone ballast, laid to a stated depth of eighteen inches under the sleepers is used.

With an expert eye, Major Pringle had noticed that, 'in certain places the ballast was somewhat insufficient in quantity', and he added that this would have to be remedied.

Small platforms had been erected intermediately between Northam and Appledore at Richmond Road and at Lover's Lane. Richmond Road was furnished with a small shelter for waiting passengers, but Lover's Lane was without shelter of any kind. Both of these minor halts had raised platforms standing one foot above rail level; these facilities were adequate for a light railway but the Inspector pointed out that, if used after dark, the two halts would also need platform lighting.

Having briefly mentioned the intermediate stopping places the BoT Inspector turned his attention to the terminal station at Appledore. In contrast to the halts at Richmond Road and Lover's Lane, the terminus was equipped with a full length passenger platform and many other facilities.

> A single platform is provided at the terminus 300 ft in length. The station building comprises a small booking office, and general and ladies' waiting rooms, together with conveniences for both sexes.
>
> A run-round loop is provided. At the buffer stop end of this loop a trap point is necessary at the fouling point with the platform road; this can be worked by the same lever which works the loop points.
>
> Home and starting signals are provided, and ground signals I understand will be arranged.

The station was equipped with a signal box containing 10 levers, including one spare. The box was linked by telephone to Westward Ho! and

Major Pringle explained that the intervening single line section would be worked by train-staff-and-ticket, trains being signalled by telephone in accordance with an agreed code.

In connection with this mode of operation the train staff section between Westward Ho! and Northam would be extended to Appledore, so that there would 'not be an additional section'. At Northam the loop and siding points had (in Major Pringle's words) 'been pulled up', and there remained 'only a through single line without points or signalling'.

Satisfied that the Appledore extension had been properly constructed, Major Pringle concluded his report as follows:

> Subject to the completion of the requirements noted in the report . . . and to a re-inspection of the works when so complete, I can recommend the Board of Trade to sanction this new extension.
>
> I have, etc.,
> J.W. Pringle, Major

There was, in fact, very little wrong with the Appledore extension line, and the minor changes demanded by Major Pringle were soon carried out. However, the line was not opened for several more days – this short delay presumably being necessary because signalling and telephone equipment had to be moved from the redundant signal box at Northam to the new cabin at Appledore.

Opening to Appledore

The line was finally opened on 1st May, 1908, on which day the Bideford, Westward Ho! & Appledore Railway was completed throughout its full length of seven miles and four chains.

Opening Day was celebrated in considerable style by the inhabitants of Appledore, and *The North Devon Journal* reported that the official 'First Train' was received by the new station master, Mr H.R. Moody, while the new platform, new footbridge and other available spaces were crowded with interested sightseers'. Having welcomed the inaugural train, local people were 'entertained to tea by the Company' at a gathering in the nearby Public Hall in Irsha Street.

The usual celebratory speeches were made, and the Vicar of Appledore proposed 'Success to the Bideford, Westward Ho! & Appledore Railway'. Other speakers referred in glowing terms to the many benefits that would accrue now that the railway was open throughout to Appledore, and it was confidently predicted that a 'huge influx of visitors' would bring wealth to the town.

These sentiments, although entirely understandable, were somewhat over-optimistic in relation to likely traffic flows on the extension line. If the BWH&AR route had been physically connected to the national railway system there might indeed have been a sudden influx of summer visitors, but in practice, tourists or holidaymakers wishing to take rooms in Appledore were more likely to arrive at the LSWR station at Bideford East-the-Water and then proceed by road directly to their destination; there was little incentive to travel the long way round via Westward Ho! when the road journey from Bideford to Appledore was barely two miles!

For similar reasons, the limited numbers of people who lived in Appledore and worked in Bideford are unlikely to have sat for half an hour in a BWH&AR train when they could have walked or ridden to Bideford. The new extension line was, however, an attraction for holidaymakers staying in Westward Ho! who could (for example) travel to Appledore on the railway and then stroll back to their hotels or guest houses across Northam Burrows.

In truth, there was little need for a railway from Bideford to Appledore via Westward Ho! and Cornborough, but this melancholy thought was far from the minds of those celebrating the completion of the railway in May 1908. What mattered then was simply that the project had been successfully completed, and those who had struggled for so long to secure a rail link could only wait and see what – if any – traffic materialised on this northernmost extremity of the Bideford, Westward Ho! & Appledore Railway.

A Bell Punch ticket issued on the BWH&AR line.

A single-coach train near Strand Road Halt. The locomotive is probably *Kingsley*, while the coach is a brake composite.
R.W. Kidner

An early view of the BWH&AR line, as a heavily-laden three-coach train rounds the sharp curves near Strand Road Halt, Bideford. *Rob Dark Collection*

Another glimpse of the line in Edwardian days, as a two-coach train heads northwards near Strand Road Halt. *Rob Dark Collection*

Chapter Four
The Railway in Operation

The completed Bideford, Westward Ho! & Appledore Railway was seven miles long, and single track throughout. Trains were able to pass intermediately in the crossing loops at Bideford Yard, Abbotsham Road and Westward Ho!, and it was theoretically possible for up and down workings to pass each other at Appledore or on Bideford Quay; Ordnance Survey maps reveal that there was, at one time, a short loop at Northam which was used for running-round purposes before the line was extended to Appledore in 1908.

Stations and Halts

Although the Bideford, Westward Ho! & Appledore line had many of the attributes of a tramway, it could boast three 'real' stations at Westward Ho!, Abbotsham Road and Appledore. Various smaller stopping places were also provided, though these were more akin to halts than stations; at Bideford, the quayside terminus had its own booking office and waiting room, as well as the dead-end goods siding which was used for occasional coal traffic.

It is unclear which BWH&AR stations handled freight traffic on a regular basis. The Railway Clearing House *Handbook of Stations* shows Bideford and Westward Ho! as 'passenger and goods stations', whereas the remaining stations were (apparently) for passenger and parcels traffic only. However, the *Locomotive Magazine* refers to 'a goods yard being provided at Northam', and there is no doubt that locomotive coal and other supplies

An up train traverses Bideford Quay as two Edwardian ladies walk their dog. The fireman can be seen standing on the right-hand side of the engine, in which position he can operate the bell mounted on top of the right-hand side tank.

Oakwood Collection

would have been delivered to Bideford Yard and Appledore in the company's small fleet of open wagons. In reality, it seems that coal was the one fairly regular source of freight traffic on the Bideford, Westward Ho! & Appledore line, and in addition to carrying its own supplies of locomotive coal from Bideford quay, the railway also carried coal from Bideford to the gas works siding at Westward Ho!.

There were, in all, up to 14 stations or halts on the Bideford, Westward Ho! & Appledore line, and these are listed in *Table One (below)*. It should be noted that the names of the halts were by no means consistent – Chanters Lane, for example, was sometimes referred to as 'The Lane', while Bideford (Strand Road) was often shortened to 'The Strand'.[23] There may, in addition, have been a number of unofficial halts or stopping places at level crossings such as Puse Hill and Mudcott crossings (both of which were near Abbotsham Road).

Most of the smaller stopping places were treated as request stops, and although one or two had platforms and waiting sheds, others had no facilities of any kind for waiting travellers. Passengers wishing to alight at the smaller halts were asked to give notice to the conductors, while people wishing to board the trains were expected to give a hand signal to the driver.

Table One

STATIONS AND HALTS ON THE BIDEFORD, WESTWARD HO! & APPLEDORE RAILWAY 1908–14

Station	m.	ch.	Type of stopping place	Facilities
Bideford Quay	0	00	street tramway terminus	G P
Bideford (Strand Road)	0	32	halt	P
Bideford (Yard)	0	40	halt and passing loop	G P
Chanters Lane	0	55	halt	P
The Causeway Crossing	0	66	halt	P
Kenwith Castle	1	75	halt	P
Abbotsham Road	2	50	halt and passing loop	P
Cornborough Cliffs	3	30	halt	P
Westward Ho!	4	55	station and passing loop	G P
Beach Road	n/a		halt	P
Northam	5	45	halt (station until 1908)	P
Richmond Road	n/a		halt	P
Lover's Lane	n/a		halt	P
Appledore	7	04	station	G P

KEY: G = Goods (including locomotive coal);   P = Passengers

One might add that, in the context of the Bideford, Westward Ho! & Appledore Railway, the difference between a station and a halt was very small. Public timetables gave the impression that Bideford, Abbotsham Road, Westward Ho!, Northam and Appledore were all stations, but in reality the only fully staffed stopping places were Bideford, Westward Ho!

BIDEFORD, WESTWARD HO! AND APPLEDORE RAILWAY.

DOWN TRAINS.—WEEK DAYS.

STATIONS.	a m.	a.m.	a.m.	a.m.	p.m.	p.m	p.m	p m.	p.m	p.m	p.m	p.m	p.m	p.m	p.m.	p.m
Bideford ...dep.	9 34	10 40	11 30	11 30	12 48	2 0	2 23	2 50	3 35	4 6	4 35	5 45	6 40	7 5	7 45	9 10
Abbotsham Rd.	9 40	10 46	11 36	11 58	12 54	2 6	2 29	2 56	3 41	4 12	4 41	5 51	6 46	*	7 51	9 16
Westward Ho!	9 49	10 56	11 45	12 8	1 3	2 15	2 39	3 5	3 49	4 21	4 49	6 0	6 55	7 17	8 0	9 25
Northam ...arr.	9 52	10 55	11 48	12 11	1 6	2 18	2 42	...	...	4 24	4 52	6 3	6 59	...	...	...

UP TRAINS.—WEEK DAYS.

STATIONS.	a.m.	a.m.	a.m.	p.m.	p.m	pm.	p.m	p.m	pm.	pm.	pm.	p.m	pm.	p.m	p.m.	p.m
Northam ...dep.	10 0	11 1	11 50	12 20	1 25	2 20	3 5	...	...	4 31	5 0	6 6	7 12	...	...	...
Westward Ho!	10 5	11 4	11 53	12 23	1 30	2 24	3 10	3 20	3 52	4 35	5 5	6 10	7 17	7 26	8 5	9 30
Abbotsham Rd.	10 11	11 10	11 59	12 29	1 36	2 30	3 16	3 26	3 58	4 41	5 11	6 16	7 23	7 32	8 11	9 36
Bideford......arr.	10 20	11 19	12 8	12 38	1 45	2 39	3 25	3 38	4 7	4 50	5 20	6 25	7 33	7 41	8 20	9 45

* This Train will not stop between Bideford and Westward Ho!   *Sunday Trains omitted.*

An early timetable before extension to Appledore.

and Appledore. Abbotsham Road, which had a passing loop and signal cabin, had only rudimentary provision for passengers (see Chapter Five), while the Causeway – which was technically a halt – was 'manned' in the sense that it had a resident signalman who lived on site and was therefore able to supervise the adjacent passenger platform.

Train Services

The pattern of train services provided on the Bideford, Westward Ho! & Appledore line fluctuated according to the time of the year, with a relatively full train service during the summer months, and a reduced timetable during the winter. In a normal summer, there could be as many as 17 trains in each direction, but in winter the service was reduced to around 10 workings each way.[24]

Two train sets were needed to maintain the service at the height of the summer. In July 1906, for example, the first down train left Bideford Quay at 9.30 am and arrived at Northam (then of course the northern terminus) at 9.53 am. It returned to Bideford at 10.04 am, reaching its destination at 10.27 am. The same train then worked an out-and-back service to Northam, leaving Bideford at 10.37 am and arriving back at 11.23 am. Meanwhile, a second train was being prepared in Bideford Yard, and it appears that this second engine and train set worked the afternoon service from Bideford Quay at 12.05 pm. There were, thereafter, two trains in operation, and these passed each other *en route* in the loop at Bideford Yard at 12.08 pm, or in the intermediate loops at Abbotsham Road and Westward Ho! during the afternoon.

The July 1906 timetable shows one or two short distance workings between Bideford and Westward Ho! while on Sundays the line was served by four up and four down afternoon trains, the first of which left Bideford Quay at 3.15 pm.

The full summer weekday service provided 17 up and 17 down trains, including 14 return workings between Bideford Quay and Northam, and three short distance return trips between Bideford Quay and Westward Ho!.

The weekday timings, in July 1906, were as shown below:

DOWN	am	am	am	pm	pm	pm	pm	pm	pm
Bideford Quay	9.30	10.37	11.25	12.05	12.55	2.00	2.25	2.51	3.15
Abbotsham Road	9.38	10.45	11.33	12.13	1.03	2.08	2.36	2.59	3.27
Westward Ho!	9.48	10.54	11.43	12.23	1.13	2.18	2.43	3.09	3.34
Northam	9.53	10.59	11.48	12.28	1.18	2.23	..	3.14	..

UP	am	am	am	pm	pm	pm	pm	pm	pm
Northam	10.04	11.01	11.50	12.30	1.25	2.25	..	3.16	..
Westward Ho!	10.10	11.06	11.55	12.35	1.30	2.30	2.51	3.21	3.45
Abbotsham Road	10.16	11.12	12.01	12.41	1.36	2.36	2.59	3.27	3.56
Bideford Quay	10.27	11.23	12.12	12.52	1.48	2.47	3.10	3.39	4.08

DOWN	pm	pm	pm	pm	pm	pm	pm	pm
Bideford Quay	3.48	4.18	4.38	5.40	6.30	7.05	7.55	9.20
Abbotsham Road	3.56	4.26	4.46	5.48	6.38	7.13	8.03	9.28
Westward Ho!	4.06	4.36	4.56	5.58	6.48	7.23	8.13	9.38
Northam	4.11	4.41	5.01	6.03	6.53	7.28	..	9.43

UP	pm	pm	pm	pm	pm	pm	pm	pm
Northam	4.14	4.50	5.05	6.05	7.00	7.29	..	9.55
Westward Ho!	4.19	4.56	5.10	6.10	7.05	7.34	8.15	10.00
Abbotsham Road	4.25	5.02	5.16	6.16	7.13	7.40	8.21	10.06
Bideford Quay	4.36	5.14	5.27	6.27	7.24	7.51	8.32	10.17

Study of the above timings will reveal that running-round at Bideford and Northam was achieved in as little as two minutes, and this raises interesting questions in terms of coal and watering requirements. There was clearly little or no time allowed for refuelling *en route*, but it seems that this problem was overcome when the second train was brought into use at midday. This train – with full bunkers and tanks – took over the operation of the line just after noon, giving the first train (which had started its roster at 9.30 am) time to return to Bideford Yard for refuelling after it had arrived in Bideford with the 11.50 am up working from Northam.

Later, with both trains coaled and watered, the first train worked a couple of out-and-back trips between Bideford and Westward Ho! at 2.25 pm and 3.15 pm, and it then formed some of the Northam workings while the second train was re-coaled and watered.

Refuelling became less of a problem during the winter months, when the train service was reduced to a basic pattern of nine up and nine down workings, with an additional train between Bideford and Westward Ho! on Tuesdays and Saturdays. This reduced timetable could be worked by just

THE RAILWAY IN OPERATION

one locomotive and one train set, with sufficient time for coaling and watering during gaps in the normal service.

The October 1906 timetable is typical of those in force during the winter months during the earliest days of the line. Operations began with the departure of the first down train from Bideford to Northam at 9.30 am, and there were, thereafter, further down services at 10.40, 11.30 am, 12.55, 2.20, 3.25, 4.25, 5.30 and 7.05 pm. In the reverse direction, the balancing up workings departed from Northam at 10.05, 11.05, 11.54 am, 1.25, 3.00, 3.50, 4.50, 6.00 and 7.29 pm.

Sunday services were not normally provided during the off-season period, though a note appended to the October 1906 timetable reveals that a limited Sunday service of two up and two down afternoon trains was run on 7th and 14th October only.

The pattern of operation established during the period from 1901 until 1908 persisted, with little alteration, after the Bideford, Westward Ho! & Appledore line was extended to Appledore in May 1908. As before, there were far more trains during the summer period than in the winter months, the summer timetable being more complex than those provided during the winter.

The July 1908 timetable provided 16 up and 16 down trains during the week and four in each direction on summer Sunday afternoons. Two trains were again needed to operate the summer weekday timetable, the first train being used to work five up and five down morning trains between 7.50 am and 2.05 pm, while the second train was brought into use at 2.00 pm, when it worked the first of a series of trains to and from Appledore. These two trains passed each other in the crossing loop at Bideford Yard at 2.02 pm, and the first train was probably refuelled after it had worked empty from

A one-coach train negotiates the sharp curve near the Bideford Technical School. The 'Armada Guns' in front of the school were used as bollards prior to the widening of the quay in 1889–90; they were in fact of English, rather than Spanish design, and although of 16th century origin they cannot have come from a Spanish warship.

Lens of Sutton

Bideford Quay to Bideford Yard at about 2.10 pm. Some of the mid-afternoon services were worked by both trains, and with two trains on the single line at the same time the loop at Abbotsham Road was brought into use for passing purposes at 4.05 and 6.50 pm, while other afternoon services passed in the crossing loop at Westward Ho! at 2.47 and 3.27 pm.

The full 1908 (weekday) summer timetable is shown below. Readers will note that most of the trains ran throughout the seven miles between Bideford Quay and Appledore, although there was one out-and-back short distance working between Bideford Quay and Westward Ho!.

Half an hour was the usual journey time for trains making the full journey from one end of the line to the other – the average speed being only 14 miles an hour!

DOWN	am	am	am	am	pm	pm	pm	pm
Bideford Quay	7.50	9.25	10.40	11.48	1.00	2.00	2.30	3.09
Abbotsham Road	8.00	9.35	10.50	11.58	1.10	2.10	2.40	3.19
Westward Ho!	8.08	9.43	10.58	12.06	1.18	2.18	2.48	3.27
Appledore	8.20	9.55	11.10	12.18	1.30	2.30	3.00	3.39

UP	am	am	am	pm	pm	pm	pm	pm
Appledore	8.25	10.00	11.15	12.28	1.35	2.35	3.15	3.45
Westward Ho!	8.36	10.11	11.26	12.40	1.47	2.47	3.27	3.57
Abbotsham Road	8.42	10.17	11.32	12.46	1.53	2.53	3.33	4.05
Bideford Quay	8.55	10.30	11.45	12.58	2.05	3.05	3.45	4.15

DOWN	pm	pm	pm	pm	pm	pm	pm	pm
Bideford Quay	3.55	4.20	5.20	5.45	6.40	7.10	8.30	9.40
Abbotsham Road	4.05	4.30	5.30	5.55	6.50	7.20	8.40	9.50
Westward Ho!	4.13	4.38	5.38	6.07	6.58	7.28	8.48	9.58
Appledore	4.25	. .	5.50	6.19	7.10	7.43	9.00	10.10

UP	pm	pm	pm	pm	pm	pm	pm	pm
Appledore	. .	4.40	5.55	6.30	7.17	7.50	9.05	10.13
Westward Ho!	4.40	4.52	6.07	6.42	7.31	8.02	9.17	10.25
Abbotsham Road	4.46	4.58	6.13	6.50	7.37	8.08	9.23	10.31
Bideford Quay	4.58	5.10	6.25	7.00	7.50	8.20	9.35	10.43

A point that might be made in relation to the July 1908 summer timetable concerns the first down train of the day, which left Bideford Quay at 7.50 am and arrived in Appledore at 8.20. These timings would have been far too late for the majority of Edwardian workmen – most of whom started work at the much earlier time of 7.30 am. One wonders, therefore, what kinds of people travelled on this first morning train? In the reverse direction the first up service arrived in Bideford at 8.55am, and this would certainly have been late for ordinary working men to have been at their daily work.

A clue to the types of passenger carried on the Bideford, Westward Ho! & Appledore line on an all-year-round basis (i.e. as opposed to summer holiday travellers) is provided by the differing natures of Westward Ho!, Bideford and Appledore. Of these three towns, Westward Ho! was unquestionably a growing residential centre, while Bideford would have provided employment for the normal range of small tradesmen and minor professional men found in a country town; it is conceivable, therefore, that shopkeepers, bank clerks, solicitors and similar 'white collar' workers would have lived in the new, brick villas at Westward Ho! and commuted to their offices in Bideford on the first up train.

In the reverse direction, varying numbers of cooks, house maids or other domestic servants would have lived in Bideford and worked in the new villas at Westward Ho!. These working class travellers (most of them females) could have used the morning down trains to reach their places of work, but for reasons stated above, ordinary working men are unlikely to have used the BWH&AR line to travel to and from work because the trains ran at the wrong times.

The only large body of workmen in the area were the shipwrights and other employees in the small ship yards at Appledore. Most, if not all of these men would have lived in Appledore, and there was, in retrospect, probably little demand for early morning workmen's trains between Bideford, Westward Ho! and Appledore; if there had been such a requirement, the railway would undoubtedly have amended its timetables accordingly, and one is left with the impression that most of the regular travellers on the Westward Ho! line must have been either Bideford office workers or domestic servants travelling to and from Westward Ho!.

The April 1910 timetable (*below*) is typical of the off-season timetables provided on the Bideford, Westward Ho! & Appledore line after its extension to Appledore. It was similar in most respects to the October 1906 timetable, the one significant difference (apart from the fact that trains now ran through to Appledore) being the presence of an earlier down train from Bideford Quay to Appledore at 7.50 am, with a corresponding up service from Appledore to Bideford at 8.25 am.

DOWN	am	am	am	pm	pm	pm	pm	pm	pm	pm
Bideford Quay	7.50	9.30	10.45	12.00	1.08	2.20	3.30	4.50	6.05	7.45
Abbotsham Road	8.00	9.39	10.54	12.09	1.17	2.29	3.39	4.59	6.14	7.54
Westward Ho!	8.08	9.48	11.03	12.18	1.26	2.38	3.48	5.08	6.23	8.03
Appledore	8.20	10.00	11.15	12.30	1.38	2.50	4.00	5.20	6.35	8.15

UP	am	am	am	pm	pm	pm	pm	pm	pm	pm
Appledore	8.25	10.10	11.25	12.35	1.43	2.55	4.15	5.25	7.10	8.18
Westward Ho!	8.36	10.21	11.36	12.46	1.55	3.06	4.26	5.36	7.21	8.29
Abbotsham Road	8.42	10.27	11.42	12.52	2.00	3.12	4.32	5.42	7.27	8.35
Bideford Quay	8.55	10.40	11.55	1.05	2.13	3.25	4.45	5.55	7.40	8.48

The normal summer or winter timetables were supplemented as necessary by the provision of special trains from dances, fêtes, gymkhanas or other events, and on these occasions all three of the railway's 2–4–2T engines would be in steam at the same time. Public holidays such as Whit Monday and August Bank Holiday were especially busy, with as many as 25 trains in each direction instead of the normal summer season maximum of 16 up and 16 down workings.

The Locomotives

The Bideford, Westward Ho! & Appledore Railway owned just three locomotives throughout its brief life, and as we have seen, these were 2–4–2 side tanks built by the Hunslet Engine Company of Leeds in 1900. The engines, which bore the names *Grenville* (Works No. 713), *Kingsley* (Works No. 714) and *Torridge* (Works No. 715) were of identical design and appearance. They had 12 in × 18 in. outside cylinders, and their weight in working order was 27 tons.[25]

Their basic dimensions were as follows:

Cylinders (outside)	12 in. × 18 in.
Driving wheel diameter	3 ft 3 in.
Leading wheel diameter	2 ft
Trailing wheel diameter	2 ft
Total heating surface	444 sq. ft
Working pressure	140 lb. per square in.
Water capacity	500 gallons (in side tanks)
Coal capacity	18 cwt
Total weight	27 tons
Coupled wheelbase	5 ft
Total wheelbase	16 ft 6 in.
Estimated tractive effort	6,978 lb. at 75%

The two cylinders were inclined slightly downwards, and the connecting rods acted upon the rear pair of coupled wheels. The leading and trailing wheels were mounted on pony trucks with sufficient side play to enable the engines to negotiate curves as sharp at 160 ft radius.

Externally, one of the most noticeable features of the three BWH&AR engines were their prominent side and end skirts which were originally fitted to comply with Board of Trade tramway regulations. In theory the skirts completely covered the wheels and motion, but in service the engines usually ran with part of the side skirting removed – this was probably necessary for oiling and day-to-day maintenance purposes.

Precise livery details are by no means clear, although the Bideford, Westward Ho! & Appledore engine livery was probably dark green, with black chimneys, smoke boxes and cab roofs. Domes and safety valve covers were of brightly-polished brass and, in earlier years at least, the three 2–4–2Ts were fully lined out in yellow or off-white. Lining was applied to the side tanks, cab sides and rear, and wheel skirting, while buffer beams and shanks were painted bright red.

The maker's plates were attached to the sides, and towards the rear of the side tanks, while the BWH&AR numbers were displayed on similar, oval-

A maker's photograph of engine No. 2, before the locomotive was fitted with side and end skirting. *Oakwood Collection*

An interior view in one of the company's third class vehicles. *Rob Dark Collection*

shaped plates mounted towards the front of the tanks. The maker's plates sported the legend 'The Hunslet Engine Comp', together with maker's numbers and the year of manufacture; the word LEEDS was proudly emblazoned on the centre part of the plates. The number plates carried the initials 'BWH&AR' and the year '1900', together with the appropriate numbers '1', '2' or '3', which were displayed at the very centre of the oval plates.

The engines carried no other signs of ownership, though the names *Kingsley, Grenville* or *Torridge* were displayed on the sides of each engine between the maker's and number plates. However, these names are not visible in contemporary photographs, and it is possible that the engines ran without their names for several years. Alternatively, the names may have been applied in blue, or some other colour which may not have shown up in Edwardian photographs – in this context it is worth pointing out that early 20th century films and plates were 'colour-blind' (or orthochromatic) films which were insensitive to certain colours.

The Bideford, Westward Ho! & Appledore engines carried small bells on their right hand side tanks, and these were rung by the firemen who stood on the front of the engines when running through the streets of Bideford.

The BWH&AR locomotives had just one lamp bracket at front and rear – the normal headcode being a single oil lamp below the chimney (or on the rear of the cab when running in the opposite direction). Cow catchers were fitted at the front and rear, and there were small tool boxes on the front right-hand side of the running plates. The engines were equipped with centre buffers and screw couplings, together with connections for the vacuum brake.

Coal was carried in bunkers situated on top of the side tanks. Large rear bunkers were never provided, and for this reason the BWH&AR engines could carry only 18 cwt of coal.

The overall appearance of the three Bideford, Westward Ho! & Appledore engines was somewhat curious. Their fully-enclosed wheels and motion imparted a decidedly box-like effect which was lessened, only slightly, when a portion of the side plating was removed. Moreover, the engines had relatively small boilers, and when viewed from the front their running plates seemed abnormally wide; there was, in fact, ample room for the firemen to stand at the front of the locomotives as they were required to do when running on the street tramway section at the Bideford end of the line.

The three engines were always well groomed, and they must have looked very smart in their fully-lined livery with the sunlight glinting on polished brass and metalwork. Labour was cheap in the Edwardian era, but this factor was not the only reason why locomotives and other equipment was always so well cleaned and maintained; one senses that most, if not all railwaymen displayed a pride in their work that is today almost totally forgotten, and this pride was as evident on minor lines such as the Bideford, Westward Ho! & Appledore Railway as it was on great railways such as the London & South Western or the Midland railways!

Before leaving the subject of BWH&AR locomotives it is worth noting, if only on a footnote, that when the three engines were delivered in 1901 they were placed on the track facing in opposite directions. Two of the locomotives faced Appledore while one faced Bideford – the odd man out being *Torridge*, which ran 'backwards' for all of its working life on the Westward Ho! line.

Passenger Rolling Stock

The Westward Ho! line had no more than six passenger vehicles, but these were adequate in relation to normal traffic requirements on this seven mile line. There were two different types of passenger vehicle on the Bideford, Westward Ho! & Appledore Railway, the first four coaches being composites while two further vehicles were third class coaches.

The original coaches, built by the Bristol Wagon & Carriage Works, were relatively large vehicles,[26] and at a time when most minor railways and branch lines were worked by short-wheelbase compartment stock, travellers on the BWH&AR route were offered the comfort and spaciousness of American-style bogie coaches.

These American-style cars were over 45 ft long, and with a generous internal width of 9 ft, they must have seemed huge to contemporary travellers. Internally, the coaches were divided into two compartments, one of which seated 40 third class travellers while the other provided comfortable accommodation for 10 first class passengers. The vehicles were entered via end platforms, and a central gangway provided access between the two rows of tram-type seats. Steps were fitted at each side so that travellers could alight or disembark at the BWH&AR's low platforms (or on the quay at Bideford) and the vehicles were illuminated by acetylene gas.

The Bideford, Westward Ho! & Appledore coach livery was polished teak, with the name of the company displayed in full beneath the windows of each vehicle and the Bideford coat of arms on the side panels. The words 'First Class' and 'Third Class' were shown on the appropriate ends of each of the composite coaches, but there does not appear to have been any obvious numbering system, and no fleet numbers can be discerned on any photographs of BWH&AR rolling stock.

The insides of the coaches were panelled in polished oak with teak mouldings, and the ceilings were covered in pale green Lincrusta Walton picked out in gold. The seats, which were reversible, were 'nicely upholstered with rep in the third class' and American leather in the first class saloons. ('Rep' was a textile fabric incorporating a corded surface.)

Like most other Bideford, Westward Ho! & Appledore rolling stock, the four composite coaches were equipped with centre buffers, screw couplings, and vacuum brake connections. When first delivered to the railway in 1900 they had also been fitted with side chains, but this archaic feature seems to have been removed at an early date.

The BWH&AR composite coaches were 45 ft long between their end platforms, the maximum length from buffer to buffer being nearer 48 ft. The most remarkable feature of their construction was, however, their extreme width of 11 ft 3 in. This was, needless to say, much wider than usual – even by present day standards; it is worth noting that the maximum width permitted on the generously engineered Great Western Railway was only

9 ft 7 in., while normal British passenger rolling stock was rarely wider than 9 ft.

The freakish width of the Bideford, Westward Ho! & Appledore vehicles can be explained, at least in part, by reference to their projecting side steps (which had been criticised by the Board of Trade Inspector in 1901). These steps were altered slightly to reduce the danger to pedestrians on Bideford Quay, but this modification is unlikely to have reduced the width of the coaches by more than two feet, and they would *still* have been much wider than most other vehicles running in Edwardian Britain.

Some further particulars of the four BWH&AR composite coaches are given in tabular form below.

Gauge	4 ft 8½ in.
Length of vehicles between end platforms	45 ft
Length between centre buffer/couplings	48 ft
Distance from bogie centre to bogie centre	28 ft
Rigid wheelbase of each bogie	6 ft
Diameter of wheels (on tread)	3 ft 1 in.
Clear width inside passenger saloons	9 ft
Maximum width over side steps	11 ft 3 in.
Height from floor to under side of roof	7 ft 3 in.
Passenger accommodation	40 third class plus 10 first class
Lighting	acetylene gas
Livery	polished teak
Builder	The Bristol Carriage & Wagon Works

The two Bideford, Westward Ho! & Appledore third class coaches were similar, though by no means identical to the four composite vehicles. Like the composites, they were large bogie coaches with American-style end platforms instead of side doors. Passengers entered the interior saloons by means of projecting steps, and a centrally-placed gangway ran longitudinally between two rows of reversible tramcar-type seats.

The four original BWH&AR coaches had 18 windows on each side, and their lower panels were covered with vertical match boarding. The two third class coaches, in contrast, had smooth side panels and larger, rectangular windows. They had a more robust appearance than the four composites, and with an overall length of approximately 60 ft they were also somewhat larger.

Some, though not all, of the Bideford, Westward Ho! & Appledore passenger vehicles were equipped with small brake compartments from which the conductor-guards could work the vacuum brakes. In the case of the composites these brake compartments were situated at the rear of the third class saloons, the coaches concerned being fitted with windows in their rear bulkheads, whereas the ordinary non-brake vehicles had no windows at either end. It was originally intended that the railway would be run with two-coach trains in the summer, and one-coach trains in the winter, the usual summer formation being one composite plus one brake composite vehicle. If, for any reason, no brake vehicle was available, an ordinary four-wheel goods brake van was coupled to two composite coaches.[27]

A maker's photograph of one of the BWH&AR bogie composite coaches. These vehicles sported an attractive polished teak livery. Note that no numbers are displayed on the exterior of the vehicle.

Oakwood Collection

An enlargement of the photograph shown on page 1 produces this useful three-quarter view of a BWH&AR composite coach. The centre buffer/coupling can be clearly seen. The conductor, in his peaked uniform cap, stands beside the train.

Lens of Sutton

The situation regarding brake compartments in the third class rolling stock is less clear-cut, but on balance it is likely that at least one (and probably both) of the third class coaches were brake thirds. Photographs reveal that in later years single coach trains were usually composed of an engine plus one third class vehicle, and this mode of operation implies that the coaches in question must have had brake compartments (or at least some provision for the guard to work the brakes).

In June 1917 *The Railway Magazine* printed a short article on the Bideford, Westward Ho! & Appledore line, and this article contained the following brief description of the BWH&AR passenger vehicles:

> The cars are long ones, somewhat of the tramcar type, but considerably bigger, and are entered from end vestibules, with steps down to road level. Two generally constitute a train, reduced to one when that will suffice, but at the height of summer three or four may be necessary . . . Rolling stock is of semi-open type or can be closed in for winter use. Some of the vehicles have double-faced clocks fitted in the cross members spanning the course of the roof.
>
> There are six passenger cars, one brake van, and eight goods vehicles. Passenger coaches are generally very comfortable, and fitted with acetylene lighting. They have centre couplings combined with the buffers.

A later article, printed in *The Bideford Gazette* on 16th February, 1937, quoted a former BWH&AR guard, who recalled that the average number of people carried on each train 'would be about 200, but that was in summer' when two-coach trains were employed; in winter 'only one coach was needed'.[28] The three-coach trains referred to by *The Railway Magazine* would probably have been needed on special occasions such as August Bank Holidays – though one wonders how the diminutive BWH&AR 2–4–2Ts could have coped with *four* coaches on the 1 in 40 gradients between Abbotsham Road and Westward Ho!.

BWH&AR Goods Rolling Stock

The eight Bideford, Westward Ho! & Appledore Railway goods vehicles appear to have been four-plank 'opens' with centrally-placed drop doors on each side. They were of conventional appearance, with 'L' shaped angle irons at each corner and diagonal bracing on the sides.

The wagons were fitted with primitive hand brakes which, from photographic evidence, incorporated just one brake shoe and one brake lever – in other words, only one of their four wheels was braked. The solebars were not protected by springs of any kind, and there was therefore no means of shielding the brake lever from the shock of the heavy side doors dropping open.

The usual Bideford, Westward Ho! & Appledore centre buffer/couplings were provided, and the goods vehicles were lettered 'BWH&AR' in small white letters. These letters (which were applied to the second plank from the top) were arranged in two groups, 'BWH' being positioned on one side of the drop doors while '&AR' appeared on the other.

It was usual, on some light and narrow gauge railways, for goods rolling stock to be pressed into service as open passenger vehicles during the

Another useful (and exceedingly rare) photograph, showing the BWH&AR brake van and two of the company's open wagons in the siding at Appledore. Note the curious, single-post buffer stop.

L.G.R.P., Collection of D.J. Powell

summer season. On the Leek & Manifold Railway, for example, two bogie goods vehicles were specifically designed for use as auxiliary summer-season passenger vehicles, for which purpose they could be rapidly fitted-up with seats and canopies. This expedient was not, however, possible on the Westward Ho! line for the simple reason that the ordinary BWH&AR goods vehicles were not fitted with vacuum brakes, and they would not, therefore, have been suitable for employment as summer passenger rolling stock.

There was, in addition to the eight goods wagons, a four wheel brake van which, being vacuum fitted, was intended for either passenger or goods use. This vehicle was, in its external appearance, something of a hybrid; it had two end verandahs like a normal brake van, but whereas conventional goods brake vans were fitted with projecting look-outs on each side, the BWH&AR van was equipped with pairs of sliding doors. The brake van was, in effect, a combined brake vehicle plus goods van, and small parcels and sundries traffic could conveniently be carried in what would normally have been the guard's compartment.

The brake van had gates in the centre of its two verandahs, and when running in formation with passenger vehicles the guard was able to walk through these gates and onto the end platforms of the passenger stock.

In contrast to the ordinary open wagons, the brake van was equipped with four brake shoes that acted on each wheel – the guard's brake handle being fitted at the end of one of the verandahs. The vehicle was lettered 'BWH&AR' in small white letters which were positioned on the sliding side doors.

Details of the Bideford, Westward Ho! & Appledore goods livery are elusive, but by analogy with other Edwardian railways the eight BWH&AR open wagons are likely to have been painted either brown or grey. Photographs reveal that the goods brake van was painted a lighter colour, which may have been light grey. On the other hand, as the brake van was originally intended to run in formation with the passenger vehicles it may have been finished in the BWH&AR passenger livery of varnished wood. (When, in later years, this varnish started to wear away, the natural wood colour would have become more pronounced, and this may explain the difference in shade between the brake van and the open wagons.)

Goods trains on the Bideford, Westward Ho! & Appledore line were probably run on an 'as required' basis. The unfitted open wagons could easily have been attached to the rear of normal passenger trains, though it is perhaps more likely that the regular movement of coal between Bideford Quay and Westward Ho! gas works was carried out by special goods trains consisting of one or two open wagons and the BWH&AR brake van. Additionally, the goods rolling stock would have been sporadically used for the movement of sleepers or other permanent way materials, and in this context it is important to remember that all tramways and passenger-only railways needed a small fleet of 'service' vehicles (London Transport being a good example of a passenger-orientated undertaking with a large fleet of 'goods' vehicles for engineering use).

Signalling Notes

Although there have already been several references to signalling matters in earlier chapters, it would be worth adding a few extra details, and the following notes (which should also be read in conjunction with the 'route' section in Chapter Five) may be of interest to readers seeking a further insight into the operation of the Westward Ho! line.

Like all single line railways, the Bideford, Westward Ho! & Appledore line was worked by a single line staff, the route from Bideford to Appledore being divided into four 'staff sections' as recounted in Chapter Two. As the Westward Ho! line was a holiday route that sometimes carried many extra summer trains, it was necessary for the train staff to be made 'divisible' so that (for example) two or more successive trains could proceed from Bideford Quay to Westward Ho!. This was achieved through use of the train-staff-and-ticket system, which worked as follows; the first train to leave Bideford Quay departed after the driver had been shown the train staff, and although the actual train staff remained at Bideford in the hands of the Traffic Manager (or other responsible person) the driver of the first train was given a small 'ticket' as proof that he had seen the staff and been given permission to proceed. When the first train reached the next block section – in this case Bideford Yard – and the driver had handed in the ticket, the signalman on duty there telephoned the office in Bideford to say that the second train could enter the single line section. Only then could the next train proceed, and only then would the wooden train staff be taken on to the next signal box.

The above example of the train-staff-and-ticket system in operation is of course hypothetical, but it will serve to illustrate the *theory* of train-staff-and-ticket operation. In practice most BWH&AR trains were operated on the basic train staff system – the ability to introduce the 'ticket' element of operation being a useful safeguard in the event of sudden emergencies or unexpected traffic requirements.

A point that might be made in respect of the Bideford, Westward Ho! & Appledore Railway's signalling system concerns the importance of telephone communication between signal boxes. There were no block telegraph instruments, and instead the single line was worked on what should properly be called the 'manual train-staff-and-ticket principle in conjunction with the telephone'. Before despatching a train into the next single line section the signalman would telephone the next signal box in the direction to which the train was travelling to ensure that the line ahead was clear, and having thereby checked that the line was clear he was then able to allow the train to proceed.

The line was signalled with conventional semaphores, Bideford Yard and Abbotsham crossing loop being fully equipped with up and down home and starting signals, while Appledore was similarly equipped with down home and up starting signals. It would appear that Westward Ho! station was provided with home signals in the up and down direction, but no starting signals seem to have been installed; if this was in fact the case, trains would have proceeded to the next stations at Appledore or Abbotsham Road on the authority of the train staff (or ticket) alone.

Some of the level crossings at the Bideford end of the line were protected by 'home' signals in each direction, and the up home signal at the Causeway Crossing also carried a fish-tailed distant arm working in conjunction with the up home signal at the neighbouring Chanter's Lane crossing (which was only 13 chains further on). Subsidiary siding arms were employed at a few places, and there is evidence that ground discs or miniature signals were intended to be placed in the terminus at Appledore (though it is by no means certain that these were actually installed).

Miniature semaphore signals were also installed at Abbotsham Road. In this case, photographs clearly reveal that the signals in question were actually provided, though there is an element of doubt regarding their precise usage. Douglas Stuckey has tentatively suggested[29] that these miniature signals were for level crossing protection, but close study of maps and photographs indicates that the two miniature semaphores were sited, not by the level crossing but at each end of the up and down passenger platforms. Moreover, the miniature signals cannot have replaced the full-size up and down starting signals because the latter signals remained in use *after* the addition of the miniature starters; it seems, therefore, that the two small-scale signals acted as 'repeater' arms in conjunction with the main starting signals – this may have been deemed necessary because of visibility problems caused by dense foliage that sometimes obscured the normal up and down starting signals.

Tickets and Fare Collection

Tickets and fare collection are closely connected with train services, and it would be appropriate to make at least some mention of this aspect of Bideford, Westward Ho! & Appledore history.

In its 1901 opening report *The Bideford Gazette* stated that there would be no ticket offices on the Westward Ho! line because all tickets would 'be issued by the conductors of the trains'. This may indeed have been the initial intention, but at the same time there is no doubt that the Bideford, Westward Ho! & Appledore Railway had at least two booking offices on its seven mile system. The offices in question were in the BWH&AR premises at 20, The Quay, Bideford, and in the station building at Appledore.

There is sound evidence to support the contention that the Westward Ho! line had two ticket offices. Photographs clearly show that the words BOOKING OFFICE AND WAITING ROOM were prominently displayed on the plate glass windows in the front of the railway's quayside office, while Major Pringle's 1908 inspection report unambiguously states that 'a small booking office' was available at Appledore station.

It is possible that tickets were issued, not only at Bideford, Appledore and on the trains, but also at Westward Ho!. On the other hand, the vast majority of bookings are likely to have been made on the trains, and contemporary photographs clearly reveal that BWH&AR conductors carried tramway-type wooden ticket racks, from which vertical tram-style tickets were issued. As far as can be ascertained Bideford, Westward Ho! & Appledore tickets were usually of the 'geographical' kind, with lists of the various boarding and alighting points arranged on either side of the actual fares.

Most of the tickets used by the Bideford, Westward Ho! & Appledore Railway were supplied by the Bell Punch Company. This company was a major supplier of tram (and later) bus tickets, and it is hardly surprising that BWH&AR tickets resembled tram tickets rather than normal railway issues!

Interestingly, the company also employed some unusual tram-type tickets known as 'Simplex Cutter Tickets'. The Simpler Cutter system employed a sort of adjustable scale, by means of which the conductors could indicate the fare stage applicable to each booking. This system offered few advantages over the Bell Punch method of fare collection, and after using Simplex tickets for a few months the Bideford, Westward Ho! & Appledore Railway reverted to the familiar Bell Punch system.

The normal third class return ticket from Bideford to Appledore was 8d. return, but special 'market tickets' were available on Tuesdays and Saturdays at the reduced rate of 6d. and these cheap travel facilities were much appreciated by local residents.

Workmen's tickets were available for use on the first up and down trains of the day (thereby suggesting that the line carried at least *some* working class travellers); the normal workmen's return fare from Bideford to Appledore (or vice versa) was 6d. Bathing tickets were another popular feature of Bideford, Westward Ho! & Appledore operations, and these, too were sold for only 6d. return instead of the ordinary 8d. third class return. As a means of encouraging regular 'commuter' business, the railway also issued books of ten tickets which were sold to visitors or residents for 3s. 4d.

The fares charged seemed to have little relation to the scale of charges set out in the 1896 Act of Parliament – the general rule being that longer distance journeys were much cheaper than they could legally have been, while shorter distance travellers were penalised by higher fares. As the BWH&AR was allowed to charge up to 3d. per mile for first class journeys, the first class fare from Bideford Quay to Westward Ho! could, for example, have been fixed at 1s. single. Instead, the company charged just 8d. for this journey of 4¾ miles. Conversely, third class travellers from Bideford Quay to the Strand Halt (less than one mile) were charged 1d.

Some typical examples of Bideford, Westward Ho! & Appledore first and third class single fares are shown below:

Booking	1st	3rd
Bideford Quay to Westward Ho!	8d.	5d.
Bideford Quay to Chanters Lane	2d.	1d.
Bideford Quay to the Causeway	2d.	1d.
Westward Ho! to Northam	3d.	2d.
Abbotsham Road and Northam	3d.	2d.
Abbotsham Road and Bideford	3d.	2d.
Northam and Westward Ho!	3d.	2d.

The Bideford, Westward Ho! & Appledore Act of 1896 contained provisions relating to the carriage of second class passengers, but in practice the railway had no second class facilities, and only first and third class tickets were ever issued.

The writer, who has collected railway tickets for many years, has never seen a Bideford, Westward Ho! & Appledore 'Edmondson card' ticket, but this does not necessarily mean that no BWH&AR Edmondsons were issued. Through booking facilities were available between the Westward Ho! line and the London & South Western Railway, and it is possible that the Bideford, Westward Ho! & Appledore company may have issued Edmondson card tickets for outward bookings to stations on the LSWR system.

In the reverse direction, inwards bookings *from* the LSWR would have brought standard LSWR card tickets onto the BWH&AR – and to that extent it could be said that at least some Edmondson card tickets were used on the Westward Ho! line.

In addition to issuing tickets for passenger travel, the Bideford, Westward Ho! & Appledore Railway also issued parcels or sundries tickets for a variety of items. A litter of puppies, for instance, could be carried for 1s., while harps 'in or out of cases' were conveyed over the line for 2s. 6d. Dogs accompanied by their owners were carried any distance for 3d.

When parcels or other items accompanied passengers, the bookings would have been made in the normal way, and Bell Punch tickets would have been issued for the appropriate item. If, on the other hand, parcels were sent without an accompanying passenger, the railway issued special parcels 'stamps'. These were small ticket-like labels which were affixed to the parcels at the forwarding station (or possibly by the conductor). Surviving BWH&AR parcels stamps are horizontal paper tickets printed on buff or white paper; the name of the railway is shown in full, together with the amount paid.

At the time of opening the BWH&AR charged the following rates for parcels carried between any two stations:

        Weight not exceeding 7 lb. ....1d.
        Weight not exceeding 14 lb. ....3d.
        Weight not exceeding 28 lb. ....4d.

These charges included the cost of delivery within half a mile of either Bideford or Westward Ho! stations, but delivery arrangements did not exist at any of the halts; it is understood that when the railway was extended to Appledore in 1908 the delivery arrangements were expanded to take in an area within half a mile of the new terminus.

Bicycles accompanying passengers were conveyed over the railway for 6d., though if sent as 'parcels' the charge was 1s. irrespective of weight or distance carried.

PARCEL STAMP
Bideford, Westward Ho! and Appledore Railway.
3883 1d PAID

Bideford Quay showing Westward Ho train.

This view, taken from a hand-tinted postcard, shows a newly-arrived up train on Bideford Quay. The locomotive appears to be *Torridge*. *R.W. Kidner*

A further glimpse of Bideford Quay, showing a down train composed of one composite coach. *Alexander Keiller Museum, Avebury*

The Old Ship Tavern on Bideford Quay had many associations with Charles Kingsley's novel *Westward Ho!*. *Oakwood Collection*

Bideford Quay, seen from Bideford Bridge. A three-masted schooner is tied-up alongside, while a two-masted ketch can be discerned further along the quay. The Old Ship Tavern (seen on the previous photograph) can be seen to the left of the schooner. *Oakwood Collection*

Bideford Quay before the installation of the run-round loop. The line runs along the Quay, and thence around the Technical School and beside Pill Road to Strand Road Halt.
Reproduced from the 1904 25" Ordnance Survey map

An interesting close-up view of an up working on Bideford Quay. No less than six BWH&AR employees can be seen in this c.1912 view including a conductor (in cloth cap and carrying his Bell Punch ticket rack) and three footplatemen; one of the latter has removed the lamp from the front of the engine (extreme right) while his colleague walks towards the camera with a detachable lever, with which he will

Chapter Five
The Route from Bideford to Appledore

It would now be appropriate to describe the stations and route of the Bideford, Westward Ho! & Appledore Railway in greater detail, and the following chapter will take readers on an imaginary guided tour of the line as it would have appeared prior to its tragically early demise. The tour will begin on the quayside at Bideford, and then continue along the route to Appledore in the 'down' direction.

Bideford Quay

Edwardian travellers would have arrived in Bideford via the London & South Western Railway branch from Exeter to Barnstaple, which reached Bideford on 2nd November, 1855 and was extended to Torrington on 10th June, 1872. The LSWR station was, as we have seen, situated on the east bank of the Torridge in the outlying suburb of East-the-Water and, in order to reach the Bideford, Westward Ho! & Appledore line, passengers had to cross the river by foot or in horse-drawn cabs. Fortunately, the LSWR station was conveniently sited near the eastern end of Bideford's famous bridge, and for travellers without excessive luggage, the walk across the bridge to Bideford Quay could be accomplished in a matter of minutes.

On reaching Bideford proper, Edwardian visitors immediately turned right onto Bideford Quay, and after a further walk of 200 yards, they reached the Bideford, Westward Ho! & Appledore terminus. Facilities here were comparatively simple, the track layout being merely a run-round loop in the centre of the roadway. Nearby, booking office and waiting room accommodation was available on the lower floor of a building on the west side of the street – though in sunny weather travellers were able to sit in the open air on the many park-type benches which lined the quayside.

There was no station master, as such, at Bideford, but in practice Henry Sowden, the railway's general manager, was in full charge of operations at the quayside terminus. Mr Sowden, who had been station master at Blackmoor Gate (on the neighbouring Lynton & Barnstaple Railway) prior to his appointment as BWH&AR general manager, had an office beside the railway's quayside waiting room – the 'Manager's Office' being to the left while the 'Booking Office and Waiting Room' was to the right of a common entrance.

There were no signals or levers on the quayside, this part of the line being regarded as a street tramway rather than a railway; when engines ran-round their trains the points were worked on a tramway system – a long-handled metal key being employed to work the points at either end of the run-round loop. As the line ended literally in the middle of a public road, it was impracticable for a terminal buffer stop to be provided, and for this reason the railway simply petered out. There was no means of stopping runaway vehicles from continuing southwards onto the road – though in practice operations at the quayside terminus were conducted at such a slow speed that few real problems were ever experienced.

A far greater problem, from the point of view of road safety, was presented by the enforced proximity of steam locomotives and horses on a public highway. Horses were, in many ways, far more dangerous than present day

The BWH&AR booking office and waiting room on Bideford Quay. There was another booking office at Appledore, but otherwise most tickets were issued on the trains.
Rob Dark Collection

A train enters the loop at Bideford. The Kingsley Statue (erected in 1906) can be seen in the distance.
Photomatic Ltd

motor cars, and Victorian and Edwardian newspapers were full of alarming road accidents caused by excited or unpredictable beasts. There was always a possibility that horses would be startled by sudden whistles or emissions of exhaust steam – with consequent danger to other road users. Such incidents occurred from time to time on Bideford Quay, one of these mishaps being caused by the collision of a reversing train and a horse and trap.

As we have seen, relations between the railway and the Town Council – which had owned the quay since 1828 – were frequently strained. In truth, the local authorities did not want the railway on the quay at all, and in order to prevent further aggravation the railway company arranged its timetables in such a way that trains spent very little time at the quayside terminus. In general, incoming trains spent no more than five or ten minutes at the terminus, and most workings departed as soon as they had run-round.

As their trains waited briefly on the quayside, travellers were able to admire the view across the River Torridge. Bideford bridge, with its 24 ancient arches, could be glimpsed through the trees which lined the quay while, to the south, appreciative Edwardian tourists would have seen a number of interesting old inns and houses. One of these was the 'Old Ship Tavern', which had featured prominently in Charles Kingsley's *Westward Ho!* as the chosen meeting place of 'The Brotherhood of the Rose'.

When everybody was safely aboard, trains proceeded slowly along the road for a distance of about 200 yards, and having passed the entrance to Bridge Street, the single line then curved towards the right. Still running along the middle of the public road, trains soon passed the junction which gave access to the quayside goods siding. This dead-end siding extended along the outer edge of the quay for a distance of about six chains; it was long enough to accommodate all of the railway's nine goods vehicles – though as the local council objected strongly to the BWH&AR being on the quay in any shape .or form wagons were seldom parked in the quay sidings.

With Bideford Technical School now visible to the left, trains commenced a 90 degree turn towards the west which took them away from the river and onto the reclaimed 'Pill'. To the right, Charles Kingsley's statue served as an appropriate memorial to the Anglican clergyman who had done so much to place North Devon on the tourist's map, while to the left the Bideford Art & Technical School was guarded by a battery of eight 16th century ship's guns. The Kingsley Statue had been erected in 1906, while the guns had been dug up when the quay was widened in 1889–90; until that time, they had served as mooring posts for visiting vessels.

Having rounded the curve, trains ran due west, with Victoria Park to the right and Pill Road to the left; much of the land in this vicinity had been reclaimed by the railway when the line was built. The tramway section, with its distinctive wooden blocks, ended near the Technical School, and as trains continued along the Pill they ran along conventional sleepered track – although deep ballasting meant that only the tops of the rails were visible on this section of line.

Two post-closure views of Bideford Yard, showing the carriage shed (*top*) and the engine shed (*bottom*). Both of these structures spanned two tracks. The date is 9th July, 1964. *R.W. Kidner*

Bideford Yard

Strand Road, the first stopping place, was situated towards the end of the Pill, a little over 30 chains from Bideford Quay. Contemporary Ordnance Survey maps give no indication of a platform at this point, though as the steps on each side of the Bideford, Westward Ho! & Appledore passenger vehicles extended almost to the ground level passengers could easily have got on and off the trains without the benefit of a raised platform.

Now heading north-westwards, the line ran along a low embankment, and trains soon reached the operational headquarters of the railway at Bideford Yard. The Yard was not shown in timetables as an official stopping place, but it is likely that trains called to pick up or set down staff as required. There was also a need to stop here for passing purposes, and in practice 'the Yard' seems to have been one of the most widely used crossing places for up and down workings.

The track layout at the Yard consisted of a six chain loop, from which a pair of dead-end sidings diverged north-westwards to serve the railway's large carriage shed. The latter was a substantially-built structure spanning both carriage sidings. It was solidly built of local stone, with yellow-brick quoins and window surrounds; large doors in the south gable allowed rolling stock to be shunted into the building for storage or maintenance purposes, and with a length of over 100 ft, the shed was able to provide covered accommodation for up to four of the company's six passenger vehicles.

A similar, but slightly smaller building was available for use as an engine shed. This too was a twin-road structure spanning two sidings, and, like the carriage shed, the engine shed had large doors in its southern gable. One of the two locomotive sidings terminated within the shed, but the other passed right through the building and ended at a buffer stop beyond the north wall of the structure. The engine shed was sited to the north of the loop, with direct access via a siding connection that was facing to down trains.

Bideford Yard was fully signalled with home and starting signal arms, and a small 14-lever signal cabin was provided on the up side near the southern end of the loop. Other facilities in and around the yard included the usual collection of huts and storage sheds, one of which functioned as a coal store for locomotive coal.

From the Yard, northbound trains continued north-westwards and, curving gradually leftwards, they reached Chanters Lane level crossing. Like the Strand, this was the site of a request stop, and as the lane which passed over the line here was quite busy, the crossing was protected by up and down signals.

Causeway Crossing Halt

Beyond, the line straightened out as it approached the Causeway crossing. Here, some 66 chains from Bideford, the railway crossed the main road from Bideford to Northam on the level, and as mentioned in Chapter Two, the Board of Trade had insisted that a proper signal box would be required at this potentially dangerous place. There was, in consequence, a two-and-a-

The line from Bideford Yard (right) to Chanter's Lane and the Causeway. Reproduced from the 1904 25" Ordnance Survey map

half storey signal cabin beside the crossing on the down side of the line, and the crossing was further protected by up and down stop signals on each side of the gates.

The Causeway Crossing up signal also carried an additional 'distant' arm that worked in conjunction with the up signal at nearby Chanters Lane Halt; this distant (one of the very few on the BWH&AR line) was needed because Chanters Lane was barely 13 chains further on towards Bideford, and it was felt that train drivers needed advance warning in case the Chanters Lane 'stop' signal was at danger. The Causeway Crossing distant signal was distinguished only by its fish-tailed end and white chevron – yellow distant signals being a relatively late innovation dating from the 1920s (i.e. after the closure of the BWH&AR line).

The wooden gates provided at Causeway Crossing were substantially-made, with solid rectangular gate posts and a small wicket gate for pedestrian road users. There were two pairs of gates, and these swung inwards so that the line could be completely closed off to road users. Oil lamps were placed on top of the gates, and BWH&AR signalling regulations required that these should be lit at dusk, in foggy weather conditions, or during falling snow. The lights were fixed so that they showed a red light in each direction when the gates were closed across the railway, and a red light in each direction along the road when the crossing was opened for the passage of a train.[29]

To a layman, the Causeway Crossing box, with its impressive height, rows of signal levers and gate wheel, must have looked like a conventional railway signal box, and in this sense it is ironic that the Causeway box (although the most normal-looking cabin on the BWH&AR line) was merely a gate box. It was not a block post, and although the cabin was probably linked by telephone to the neighbouring signal boxes at Bideford Yard and Abbotsham Road, Causeway Crossing box was never a 'full' signal cabin in the strictest sense of the term.

The Causeway was, nonetheless, a fairly important stop for BWH&AR trains, being situated on the northern edges of Bideford, in close proximity to various new residential developments. For this reason, the Causeway was one of the more important halts en route to Appledore.

A low platform was provided for passengers on the down side of the line, and there was, in addition, a diminutive crossing keeper's cottage which abutted the east end of the wooden signal cabin. In theory, the Causeway was no more than a halt, but it is interesting to discover that Mr Fursey, who lived in the crossing cottage and worked as a gatekeeper, was known locally as 'the station master'.[30] His cottage, which was situated beside the gravelled footpath that led to the platform, incorporated a small hatch-like window, and it is conceivable that, at certain times, tickets were actually issued from this aperture (it would, for example, have made sense for the Causeway to become a 'manned' station at the height of the summer season, when the travelling conductors would otherwise have been hard-pressed to issue tickets on the trains).

The Causeway signal cabin was the largest signal box on the Westward Ho! line. It had probably been supplied by Saxby & Farmer (or some other

This well-known photograph of the Causeway Crossing is worth including insofar as it shows the raised gate cabin demanded by Colonel Yorke in his May 1901 Inspection report, and the adjacent crossing keeper's cottage. The latter building incorporated a small rectangular window which may have been intended for use as a ticket hatch. Although the Causeway gate cabin appeared to be a 'proper' signal box it was not a block post. *Oakwood Collection*

specialised signalling contractor), and its pre-fabricated timber components may well have been assembled from a variety of sources. The box was a timber-framed structure clad in horizontal weather boarding, and its upper floor was glazed with small-paned glass. A flimsy catwalk was bracketed out from the upper floor to facilitate window cleaning, and the box was heated by a metal stove; access to the operating floor was by means of an external wooden staircase at the rear of the cabin, and the roof was graced by two ornate wooden finials.

Kenwith Castle Halt

Leaving the Causeway, down trains passed through a tract of attractive Devon countryside, with a continuous belt of trees to the north and views across open pasture to the south of the line. Still heading in a westerly direction, the line climbed steadily as it followed the shallow Kenwith Valley – a small stream being discernible across open fields to the left. Passing through a small cutting, trains skirted a copse known as Raleigh Plantation, beyond which the railway emerged into open meadowland.

Westwards, the route continued past another small plantation known as Turner's Wood, and having crossed from the north to the south bank of the stream on a small bridge with steel girders and masonry abutments, trains passed over a further level crossing. Beyond, the line ascended towards Kenwith Castle Halt (1 mile 75 chains), at which point a small request stop was available for the inhabitants of surrounding farms and villages.

Precise details of Kenwith Castle Halt are elusive, though, from the evidence provided by 25 inch Ordnance Survey maps, it appears that no platform or shelter was available here. Trains simply pulled-up, if and when required, beside an ungated level crossing, and one assumes that no other facilities were ever needed.

Kenwith 'castle' was, in fact, an ancient earthwork on the north side of the railway. It was associated, in local folklore, with a battle that had supposedly taken place in 878 between a Viking raider known as Hubba the Dane and defending Anglo-Saxon forces; Hubba, who is known to have landed on the north Devon coast during the reign of Alfred the Great, is said to have been defeated under the ramparts of the 'castle', while many of his men were slaughtered in a further action at 'Bloody Corner', near Northam.

In strictly historical terms the story of Hubba's raid will never be verified, though there can be no doubt that Edwardian tourists would have been aware (from their guidebooks) of the legend attached to Kenwith Castle – and in view of this, it is perhaps hardly surprising that the promoters of the Bideford, Westward Ho! & Appledore Railway should have opened a halt beside this obscure historic earthwork!

If earlier plans had come to fruition Kenwith Castle would have been a junction station for trains to and from Clovelly, but as we have seen the Clovelly scheme was abandoned in 1901, and Kenwith Castle was destined to remain a little-used request stop throughout its 16-year existence.

A down train hurries away from the Causeway on its journey to Westward Ho! and Appledore. The up signal, with its 'stop' and 'distant' arms, can be seen in the background.
Lens of Sutton

A post-closure view of the Causeway, looking north along the road towards Northam.
Rob Dark Collection

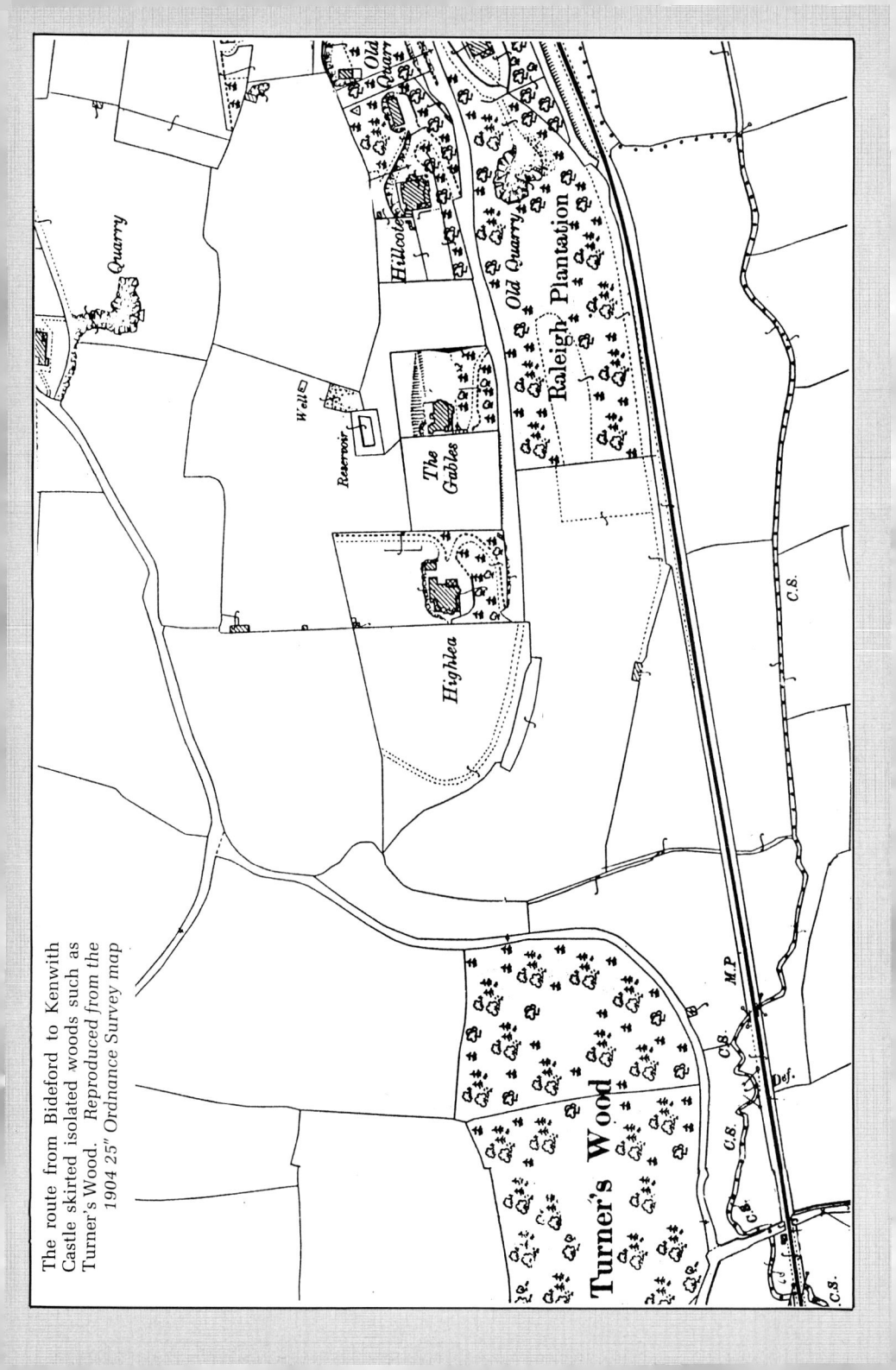

The route from Bideford to Kenwith Castle skirted isolated woods such as Turner's Wood. Reproduced from the 1904 25" Ordnance Survey map

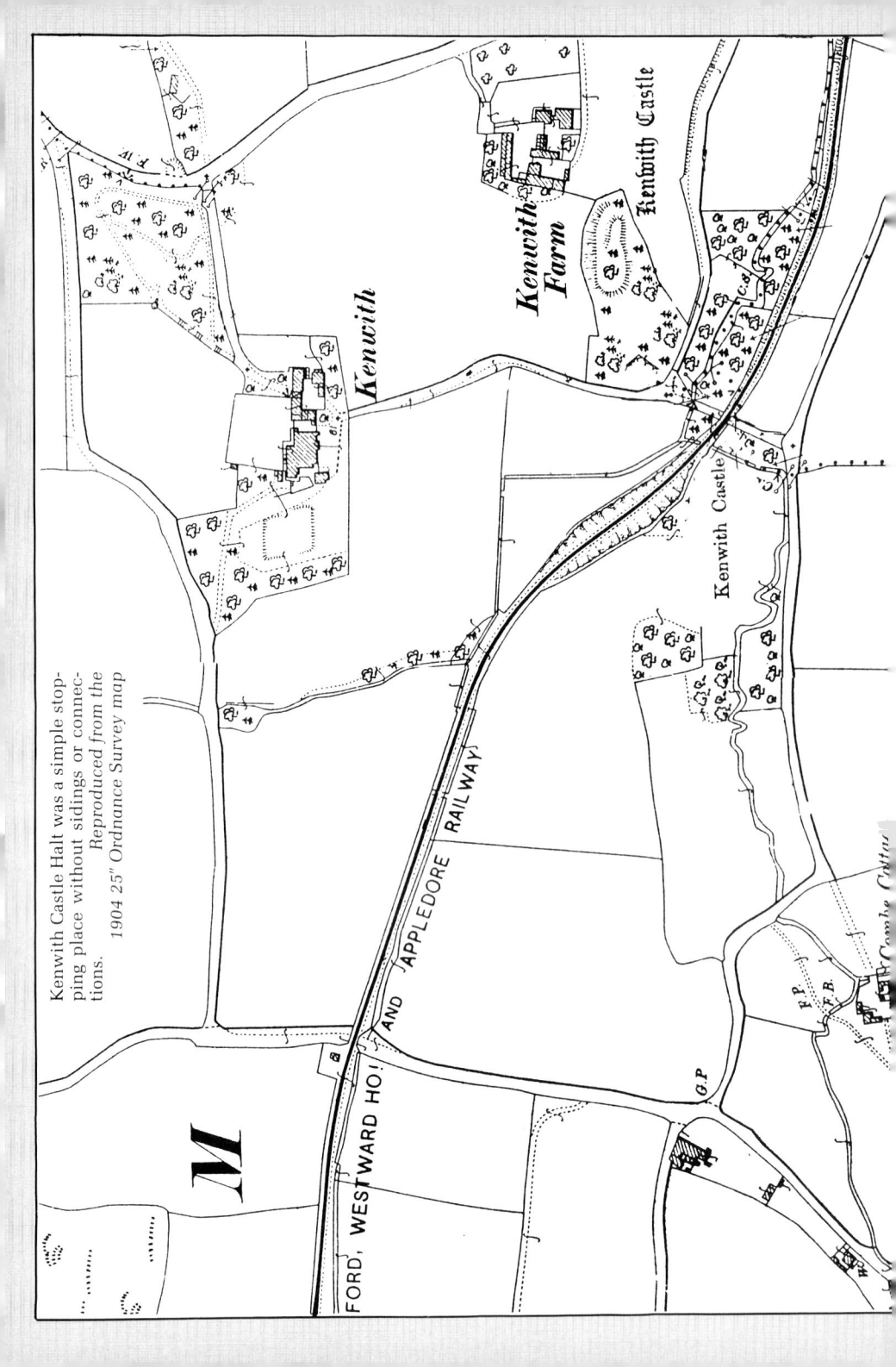

Kenwith Castle Halt was a simple stopping place without sidings or connections. Reproduced from the 1904 25" Ordnance Survey map

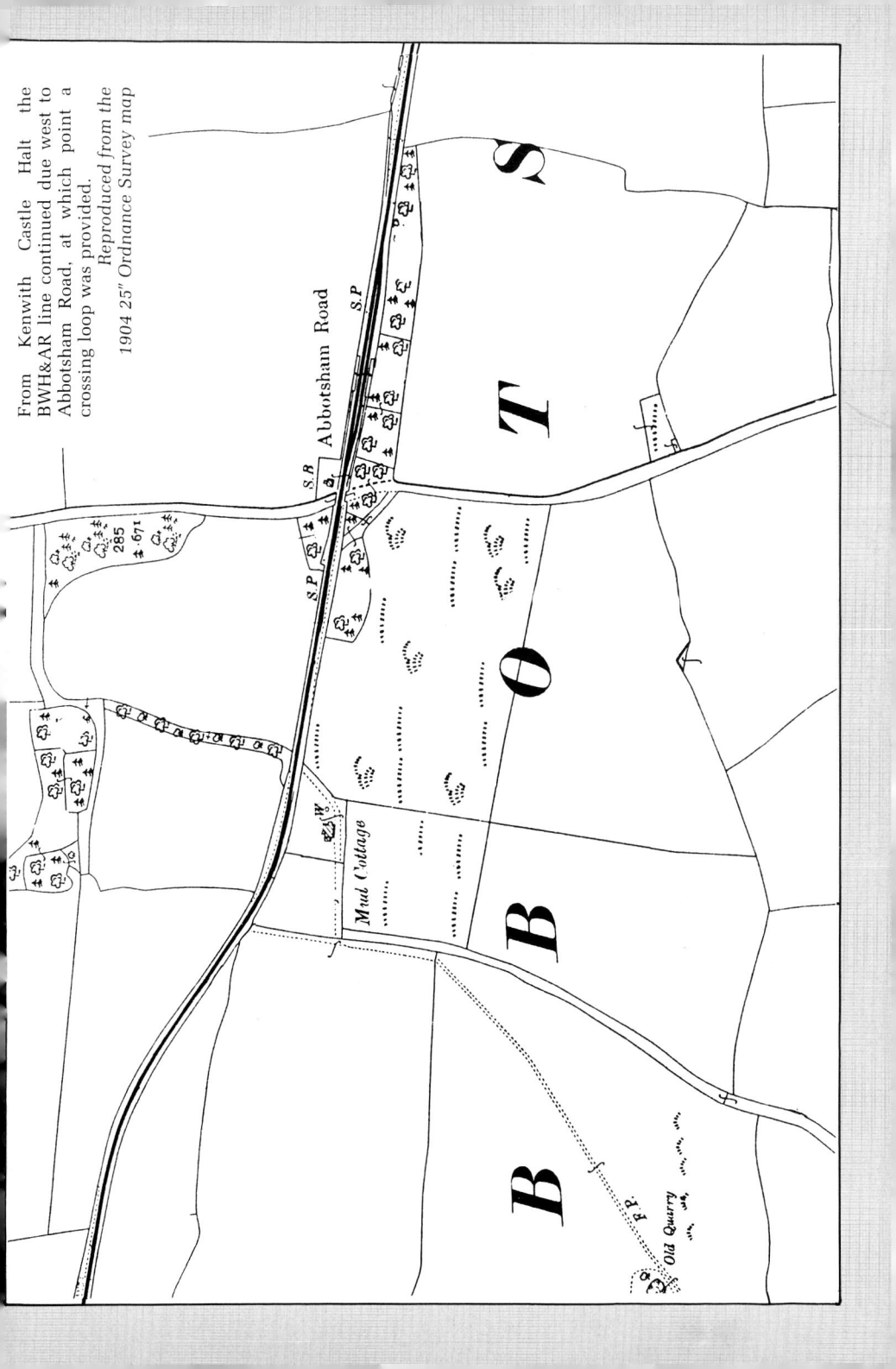

From Kenwith Castle Halt the BWH&AR line continued due west to Abbotsham Road, at which point a crossing loop was provided. *Reproduced from the 1904 25" Ordnance Survey map*

An up train departs from Abbotsham Road. The miniature starting signal at the east end of the up platform can be clearly seen, while the signal wire visible beside the running line suggests that a full-size starting signal was also employed – the miniature signal may thus have been used as a 'repeater' working in conjunction with the up starter. *Rob Dark Collection*

Abbotsham Road

Having passed Kenwith Castle Halt, the line turned north-westwards and, plunging into a relatively deep rock cutting, trains resumed their ascent on rising gradients as steep as 1 in 40. Emerging from the rock cutting the railway curved leftwards, and taking up a westerly heading once again, the route continued across sparsely-populated countryside for a further half mile.

Abbotsham Road, the next stop, was approximately 2 miles 50 chains from Bideford Quay. Perhaps surprisingly, this remote place had up and down platforms and a passing loop, together with home and starting signals and a single-storey signal box. The passing loop was a little under six chains in length, while the two platforms could accommodate just one coach each. There were no shelters for waiting passengers, though photographs show that the platforms were furnished with nameboards and simple wooden seats.

The loop seems to have been signalled for conventional up and down running, although the track itself was laid in such a way that up (i.e. eastbound) trains enjoyed a straight run through the station while down (westbound) workings were diverted over two curved turnouts.

A minor road crossed the line on the level at the western end of the loop, and this was originally protected by crossing gates; later, however, the crossing gates were removed, and in their place the line was protected by cattle guards (a similar situation pertained at several other level crossings *en route* to Appledore, many of which had their gates removed in 1905).

Contemporary Ordnance Survey maps suggest that Abbotsham Road was signalled with up home and up starting signals, while photographic evidence reveals that miniature starting signals were positioned at the west end of the down platform and the east end of the up platform; these appear to have been no more than 5 ft high, and their diminutive semaphore arms must have been about 1 ft 8 in. long.

The signals and crossing loop were worked from an eight-lever frame in the nearby signal box; when inspected by Colonel Yorke in 1901 the box had five working levers and three spares, but these arrangements were subsequently altered to provide six working signal and point levers and two spares.

Abbotsham Road was one of the most isolated stopping places on the Bideford, Westward Ho! & Appledore line – the village of Abbotsham being about ¾ mile to the south of the railway.

Cornborough Cliffs

After Abbotsham Road the character of the line changed perceptibly. Since leaving the outskirts of Bideford the route had traversed a gentle, well-wooded countryside, but after Abbotsham Road the character of the surrounding countryside became wilder, and more exposed to Atlantic gales.

Having run due west for ¼ mile, the railway reached Cornborough Cliffs,

Abbotsham Road, looking west towards Cornborough Cliffs. A miniature starting signal was provided at the end of the down platform, but no other down signal can be seen in this c.1912 view. An up home can, however, be discerned beyond the level crossing. *Rob Dark Collection*

This somewhat faded photograph provides a tantalising glimpse of Cornborough Cliffs Halt. A low platform can be seen to the right of the picture. The engine is either *Grenville* or *Kingsley*. *Rob Dark Collection*

and it then commenced a 90 degree turn towards the north-east. Emerging from shallow cuttings, trains ran along a stretch of raised embankment that was pierced, at one point, by an underline bridge or cattle creep with steel trough girders and stone abutments. Beyond, the line entered some rock cuttings and, still curving towards the north-east, down workings reached Cornborough Cliffs Halt.

Situated around 3 miles 30 chains from Bideford Quay, Cornborough Cliffs was the most remote stopping place on the Bideford, Westward Ho! & Appledore line. Facilities provided here comprised a low platform on the up side of the line – public access being by means of a footpath on the seaward side of the railway.

In the summer months Cornborough Cliffs was a popular venue for walkers and picnickers, who were able to walk along the cliffs from Westward Ho! and return later by train. In the winter, however, this part of the line was often swept by savage south-westerly gales, and Mr G. Kemp, who worked on the BWH&AR as a conductor, recalled that on occasions trains would 'practically come to a standstill' at the height of the winter gales.[31]

Running only a few feet from the cliff edge, trains followed the rocky coast past 'Mermaid's Pool' and Rock Nose, with an area of rolling hills known as The Torrs to the right, and the sea to the left. The views from this part of the line were spectacular, and on a clear day passengers could see as far as Baggy Point to the north and Hartland to the west.

Westward Ho!

At Rock Nose, the route turned onto an easterly alignment, and trains ran through a succession of cuttings and embankments as they descended towards the important intermediate station at Westward Ho!.

Falling steadily, the bustling 2–4–2Ts and their one- or two-coach trains coasted through further cuttings, and with Westward Ho! now visible on the horizon, the route finally levelled out. Running only a few feet above mean sea level, trains clattered past scattered villas and guest houses, which became more numerous as Westward Ho! station approached. Soon, hotels and rows of terraced houses came into full view, and after crossing two public roads on the level, trains drew to a stand in the down platform at Westward Ho!.

Westward Ho! was the busiest station on the line; it had up and down platforms, a passing loop, and small, but substantially-built station buildings. The station, which was 4 miles 55 chains from Bideford Quay, also boasted a signal cabin, a refreshment room, and the curiously-named 'Station Hall' with its troop of resident 'minstrels'!

Westward Ho! station had two full length platforms for passenger traffic, each of which was 320 ft long. The passing loop was a little under 8 chains in length, and as such it was more than adequate for traffic on the BWH&AR line in that it enabled two 3-coach trains to pass each other with ample room to spare. In common with Bideford, Westward Ho! & Appledore practice, the platforms were no more than a foot above rail level, though as all BWH&AR

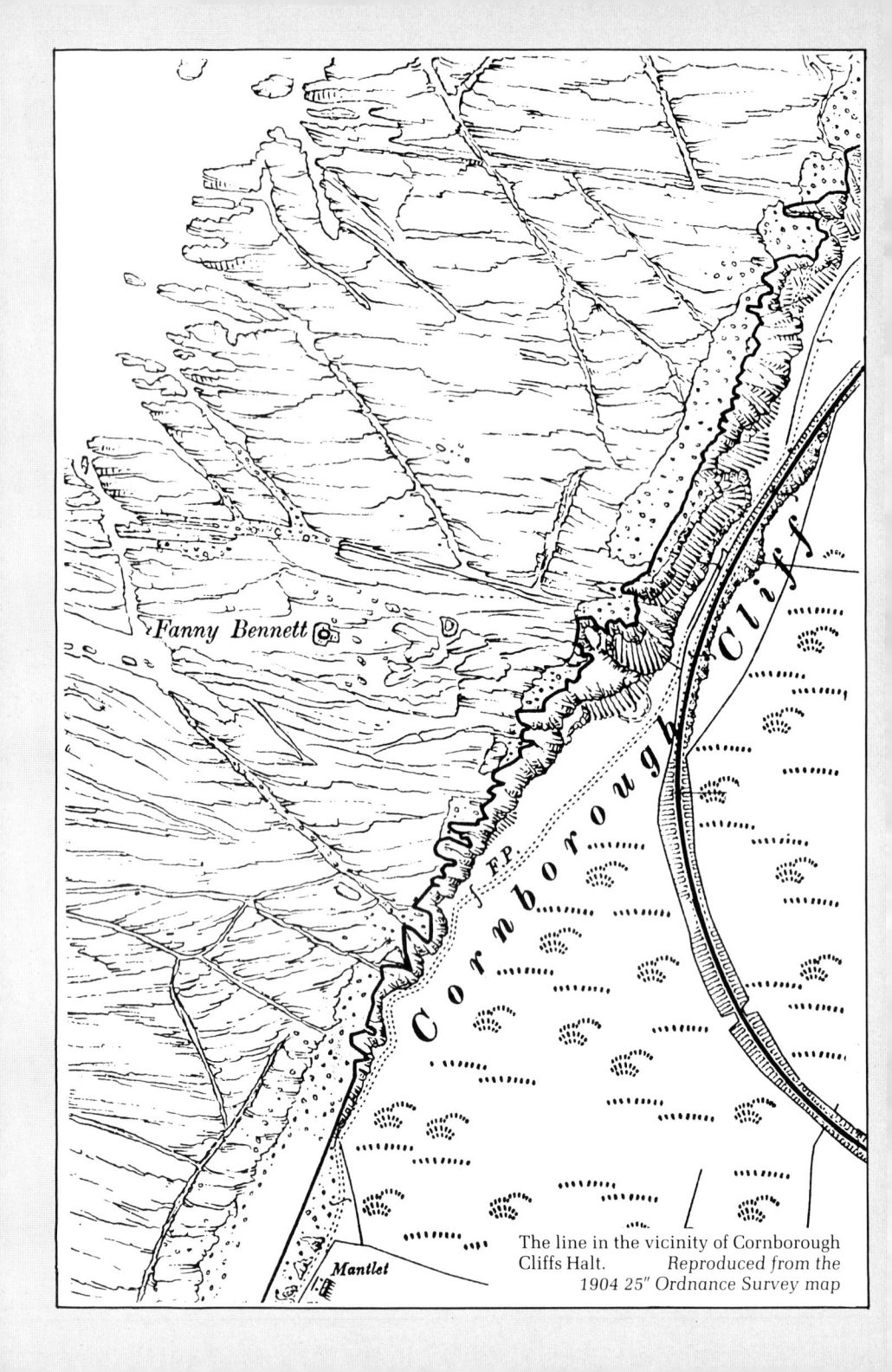

The line in the vicinity of Cornborough Cliffs Halt. *Reproduced from the 1904 25" Ordnance Survey map*

rolling stock was equipped with steps at each end these unusually low platforms would have presented few problems.

The main station building was on the up side. Of brick construction, it incorporated the usual toilet and waiting room facilities; there may also have been a ticket office – Westward Ho! being a full station rather than an unstaffed halt. The building was constructed of yellowish-white brickwork, laid in decorative 'Flemish' bonding, with regular courses of headers (bricks cemented laterally) and stretchers (bricks laid lengthways). Darker coloured bricks were used to produce a contrasting 'quoin' effect at the corners and around the windows, and the building's hipped roof was covered in grey slates.

The station building was entered via double doors that faced the platform, and there was a gentlemen's urinal at the west end. The window and door apertures were slightly arched, and the roof was graced by two ball finials that added further character to this turn-of-the-century structure.

The signal cabin, which stood on the up platform to the east of the station building, was a single storey design with a pointed roof. It may have been fabricated from parts supplied by specialist signalling contractors, but if this was indeed the case the box was clearly something of a hybrid. Internally, Westward Ho! signal cabin contained an eight-lever frame, and there was, in addition, a separate two-lever level crossing ground frame at the north end of the down platform, which was released by a key attached to the train staff of the section.

The Station Hall was situated at the west end of the up platform in close proximity to the station building. Erected in 1903, this relatively large structure supplemented the nearby waiting room in that it provided additional covered accommodation for use in wet weather. The Station Hall may also have contained extra office or storage facilities, but its main function was for summer entertainments such as dances and concert parties. A variety of artistes and performers were engaged by the railway, including black-faced seaside minstrels and the 'Dutch Doll Performing Company' – the latter being a group of entertainers who appeared before the public in Dutch national costume!

The Station Hall was a long, low single storey building, built of snecked stonework with brick quoins. Its general appearance was utterly utilitarian, the one concession to the ornamentation being the addition of somewhat incongruous ball-shaped finials on the gable ends of this otherwise undistinguished structure.

Other items of interest at Westward Ho! included a small refreshment room at the easternmost extremity of the up platform, together with the usual diverse assortment of cast iron 'penny-in-the-slot' machines, platform seats, posters, advertisements, and nameboards. The platforms were fenced with diagonal paling formed of rows of criss-crossing strips of wood, and the loop was signalled with up home and down home signals (but no 'starters').

Westward Ho! was one of the few BWH&AR stations to have its own station master, this position being filled, for many years, by Mr John Loughlin. Contemporary trade directories reveal that Mr Loughlin was also a lodging house keeper – his address being given as 3 and 4 Nelson Terrace.

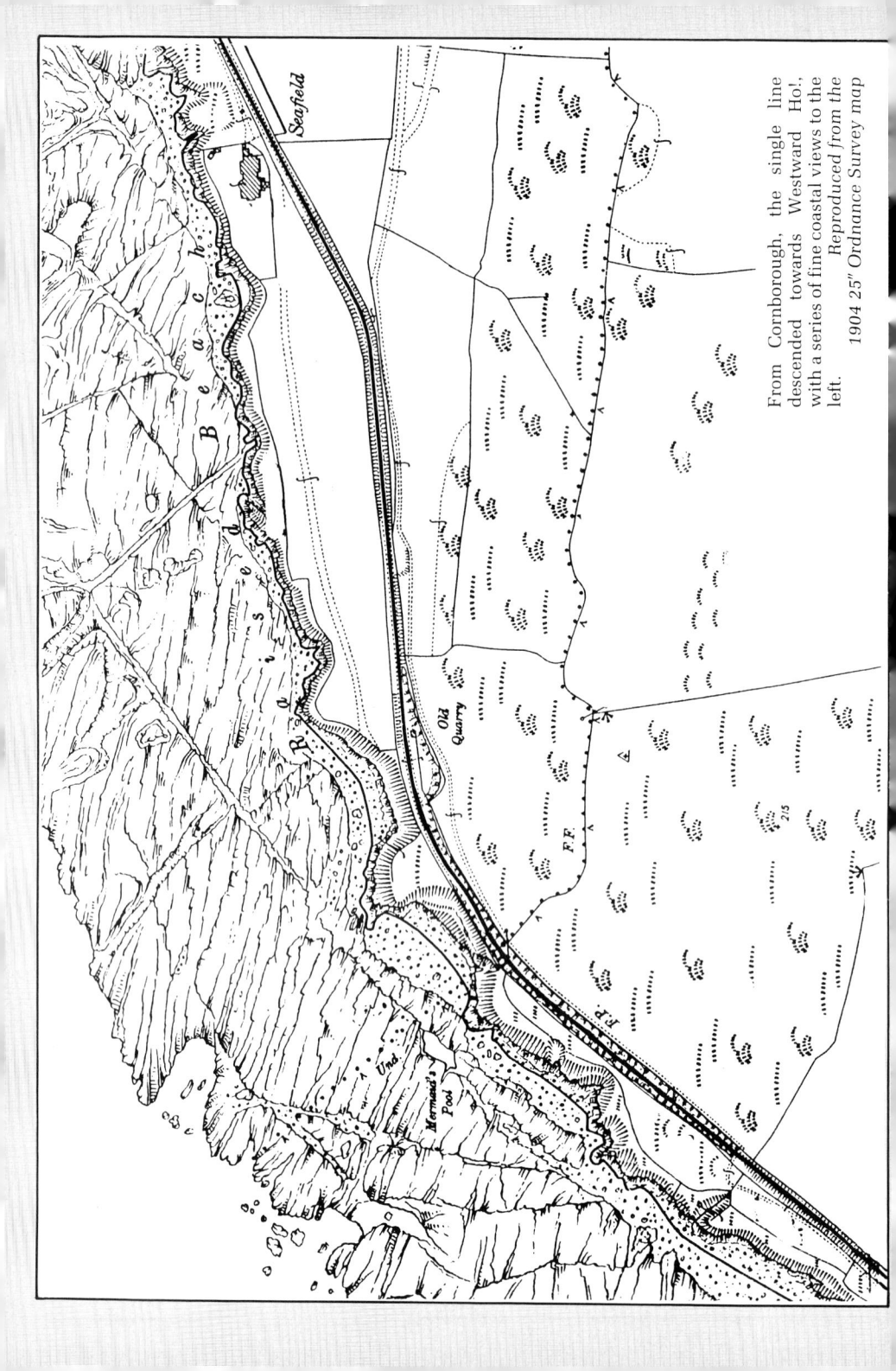

From Cornborough, the single line descended towards Westward Ho!, with a series of fine coastal views to the left. Reproduced from the 1904 25" Ordnance Survey map

A commercial postcard view of Westward Ho! during the late 1940s. The railway ran along the bottom of the hills visible behind the beach huts and bungalows of the modern resort. A cutting can be clearly seen on the extreme right of the picture.
Author's Collection

An early photograph showing a two-coach train (plus brake van) as it runs down into Westward Ho! from the Cornborough direction. The locomotive is *Torridge*.
Lens of Sutton

Later, around 1913, the station master's address was given as 'Camden', and this change of residence suggests that Mr Loughlin had prospered in his dual role of railway official and landlord!

The refreshment room at Westward Ho! station was managed by Mr F.W. Galliford who, according to *Kelly's Directory of Devon* was a baker by trade (one assumes that pies and other confections made in his bakery were sold in the refreshment room).

Westward Ho! was, in many ways, a typical Victorian speculative development which, by the turn-of-the-century, must have presented a curiously unfinished appearance. Isolated rows of terraced houses such as Nelson Terrace (to the south-east of the station) and Springfield Terrace (to the north) had been erected on some of the building plots, while in other parts of the growing settlement builders had constructed a number of somewhat larger houses and villas. There were also some large, or relatively large hotels such as the Royal Hotel, together with various churches and public buildings, a golf course, and a recreation ground. Additionally, the 'Great Nassau Baths' were available for use by townsfolk and summer visitors – passengers holding return tickets on the Bideford, Westward Ho! & Appledore Railway being admitted at the concessionary rate of 4d. per person!

Other buildings of interest included the Anglican church, which had been built in 1870, and the United Services College – which dated from 1874. The College had many associations with the poet and author Rudyard Kipling (1865–1936), who had been educated there between 1878 and 1882; the school later became the setting for Kipling's famous school story *Stalky & Co.* (1899). The United Services College had moved elsewhere by 1904, but Edwardian visitors would have been fascinated by the links between Westward Ho! and Rudyard Kipling – who was then at the height of his popularity.

The main attraction in Westward Ho! was not, however, Kipling's school, but the famous Pebble Ridge – a vast bank of smooth grey boulders that had been thrown up by the sea to the north-east of Westward Ho! station. The ridge, which extended for two miles, protected an area of pasture known as Northam Burrows, and for this reason it was regarded as incumbent on all 'Potwallopers' of Northam who exercised rights of pasture on the burrows to turn out once a year and pile up loose stones into breaches in the ridge – otherwise the sea would rapidly overwhelm the low-lying burrows. This activity was known as 'potwalloping', the term 'potwalloper' signifying those who boiled their pots 'on their own hearths' within the Northam area (in other words local householders).

Accelerating away from the down platform at Westward Ho!, trains rumbled across Golf Links Road on the level, and with Nelson Terrace to the right and Pebble Ridge visible to the left the journey to Appledore resumed.

Continuing north-eastwards, the line reached Westward Ho! gas works, at which point a dead-end siding diverged to the right; the siding, which was approximately 6½ chains long, was entered by means of a connection that was facing to down trains. As there was no run-round loop at the gas works trains probably called in the up direction only – loaded coal wagons being

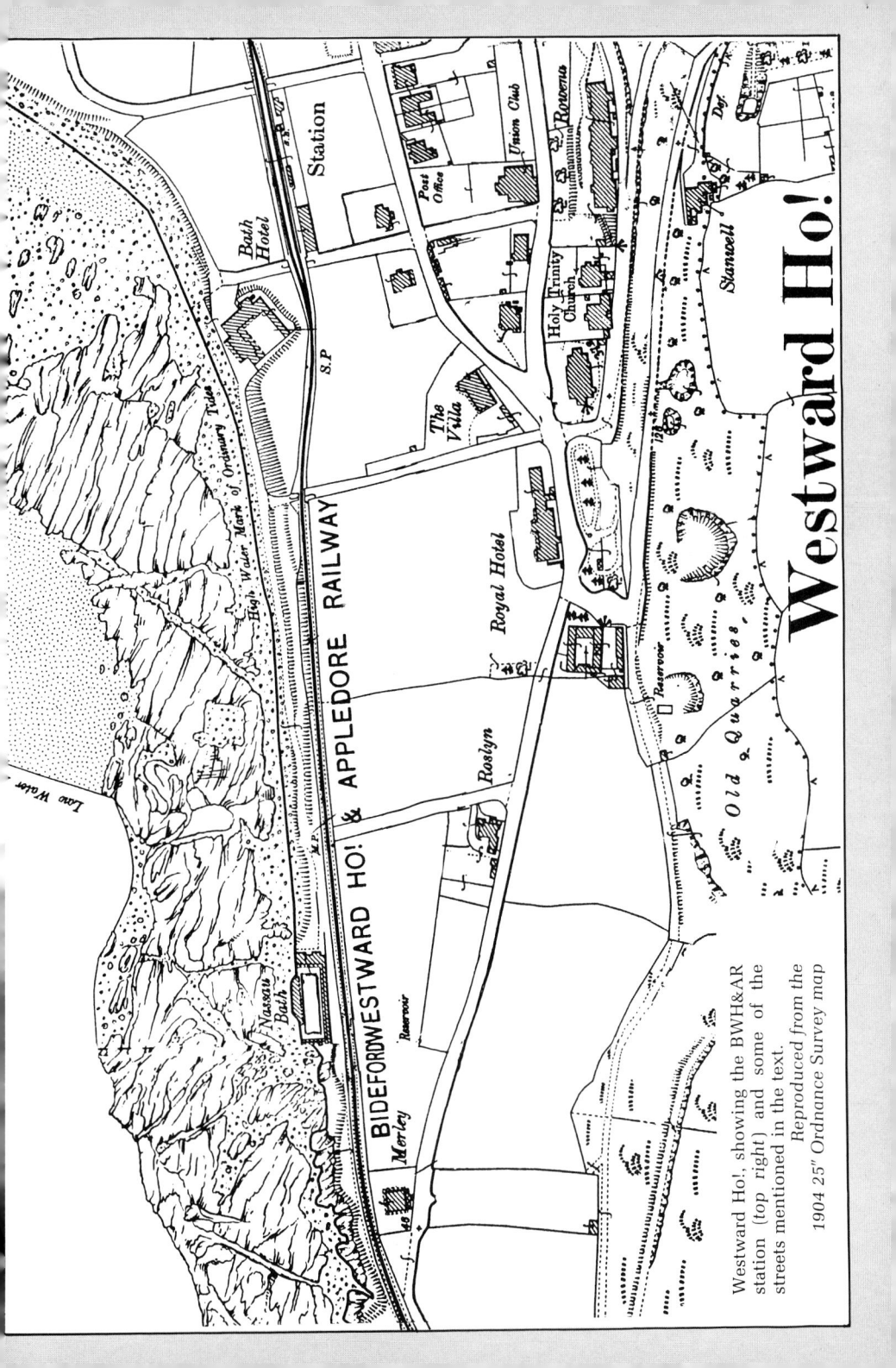

Westward Ho!

Westward Ho!, showing the BWH&AR station (top right) and some of the streets mentioned in the text. Reproduced from the 1904 25" Ordnance Survey map

Up and down workings pass in the crossing loop at Westward Ho! The coach is one of the company's two third class vehicles.

Lens of Sutton

This well-known photograph of Westward Ho! station shows (from left to right) the signal box, the station building and Station Hall. The single-storey cabin was equipped with an eight-lever frame. *Oakwood Collection*

An Edwardian postcard view of Westward Ho! (compare with the later view on *page 105*). *Oakwood Collection*

taken through to Appledore so that the siding could be shunted on the return journey. The siding was worked from a two-lever ground frame, which was released by a key attached to the train staff for the Westward Ho! to Appledore section.

Northam

From the gas works, the route continued across Avon Lane, the level crossing at this point being protected by cattle guards. Now running in an easterly direction, the railway passed groups of scattered houses and villas as it followed a level alignment towards Northam. A request stop was provided at Beach Road for the benefit of people living in Eastbourne Terrace and other outlying parts of Westward Ho!.

Northam, some 5 miles 45 chains from Bideford Quay, was usually regarded as a station, although by normal railway standards it did, perhaps, more closely resemble a halt. The 1904 Ordnance Survey map reveals that a short run-round loop was provided at that time, together with a stub-like spur or siding on the up side. However, these facilities were removed when the Westward Ho! line was extended from Northam to Appledore in May 1908, and the station's track layout was then reduced to a single line, with no turnouts or connections.

The single 180 ft passenger platform was on the down side of the line, with public access from an adjacent lane. There was a small waiting room towards the western end of the platform and, when first opened, the station had also boasted a signal box and one semaphore signal. All signalling became redundant when the railway was extended to Appledore, and the signal cabin was therefore taken out of use in 1908.

In historical terms, Northam was parochially more important than either Kenwith or Westward Ho! – indeed, the latter places were both situated within the parish of Northam. Northam village was situated about half a mile to the south of the station, and its tall church tower (which had traditionally been used as a landmark by ships entering the Torridge estuary) could be seen for miles around. Burrough House, the fictional home of Amyas Leigh in Charles Kingsley's *Westward Ho!* was situated nearby, though, by Edwardian days, this picturesque old building had been pulled down to make room for a new dwelling on the same site.

From Northam, the single line crossed Pimpley Road on the level and, turning north-eastwards, the route continued across a level tract of low lying coastal land; to the north, Northam Burrows extended towards the horizon while, to the south, newly-built villas dotted a still pastoral landscape.

At Richmond Road, trains called as necessary at a simple request stop, and having crossed further tracks or lanes on the level, the railway finally curved south-eastwards as it approached Appledore station, and the end of the seven mile scenic journey from Bideford.

Appledore

With the sea now clearly visible to the left, the route followed the tidal foreshore, Lover's Lane Halt, the penultimate stopping place, being just

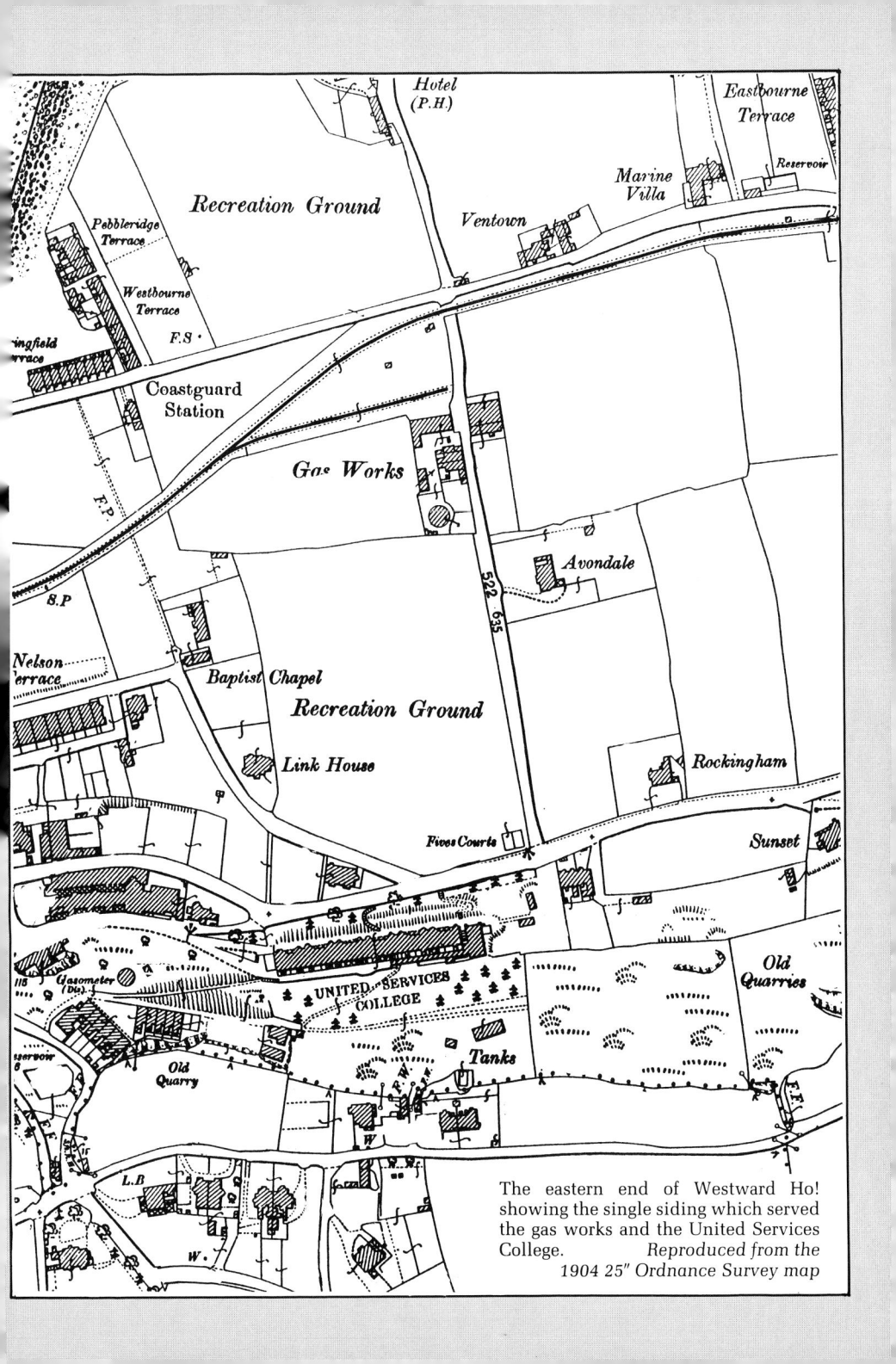

The eastern end of Westward Ho! showing the single siding which served the gas works and the United Services College. *Reproduced from the 1904 25" Ordnance Survey map*

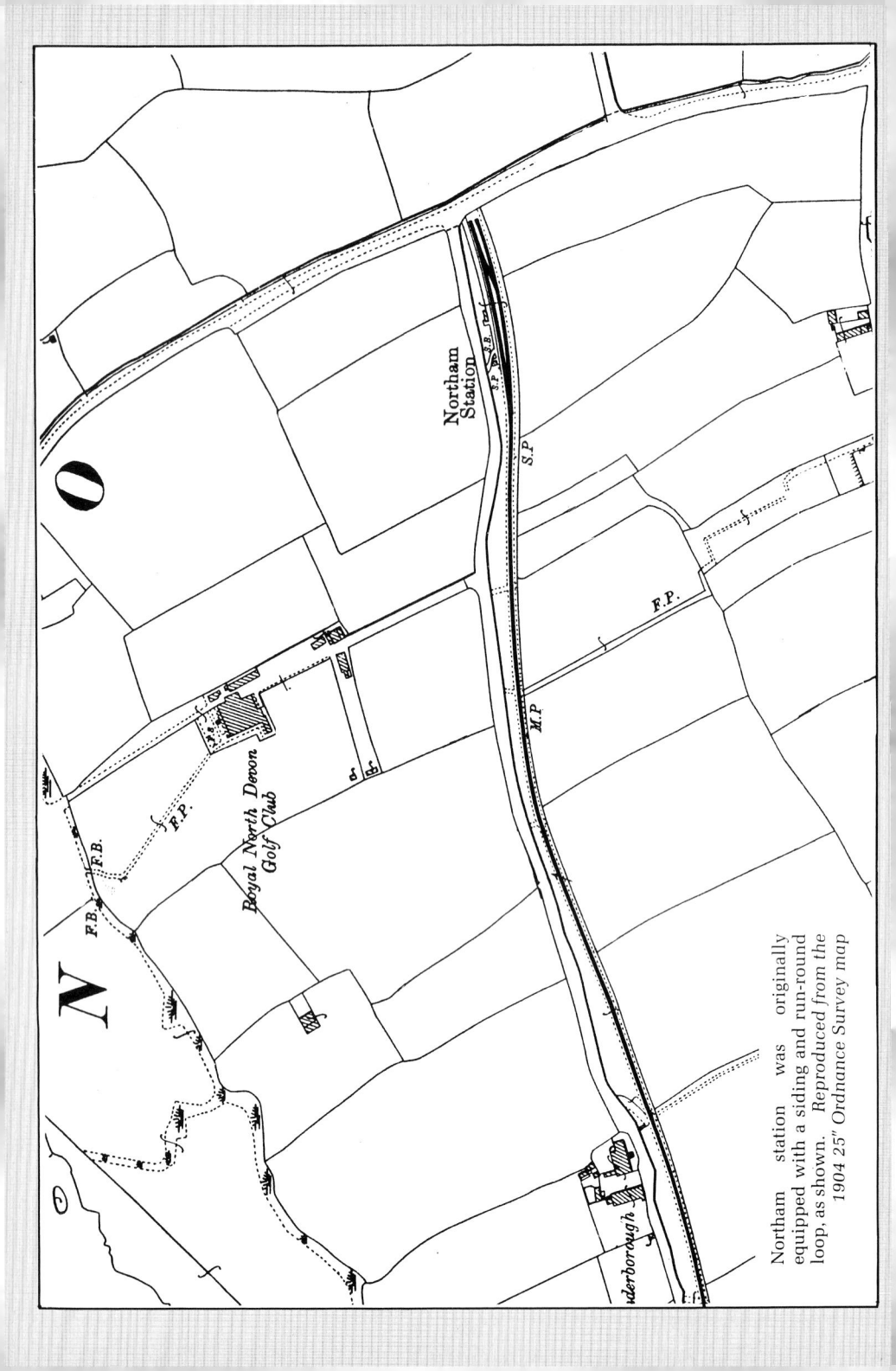

Northam station was originally equipped with a siding and run-round loop, as shown. Reproduced from the 1904 25" Ordnance Survey map

above Appledore Lifeboat station. Appledore station was only a short distance further on, and having slowed to a walking pace, trains ran parallel to historic Irsha Street for a few more yards before the line ended in a small, but neatly-built terminus near the parish church.

Appledore station was of conventional design and appearance, with a 300 ft platform on the down side of the line and a run-round loop on the up side. The loop was flanked by a long, dead-end siding that branched out near the station throat and continued parallel to the running and engine release lines before ending in a curious, single-post buffer stop; the running line, meanwhile, extended beyond the platform for a short distance in order to reach a single road engine shed at the very end of the line.

The station building was similar to that at Westward Ho!. Of brick construction, it featured a hipped roof, and slightly-arched windows and door apertures. The main external walls were formed of red brick, while contrasting yellow-white bricks were used to create a decorative effect around the doors and windows, and at the corners of the building. As at Westward Ho!, the brickwork was laid in the 'Flemish' bond style, with alternating headers and stretchers in each horizontal course.

The internal arrangements at Appledore station were similar to those at Westward Ho! in that the building contained a centrally-placed waiting room, with a gentlemen's toilet to the right (when viewed from the platform) and what appears to have been an office or mess room to the left. Unlike Westward Ho! (which was entered via double doors) Appledore station had two single doorways in its platform-facing façade; one of these provided access to the waiting room while the other gave access to the office and staff accommodation. Internal walls divided the building into three rooms – a third room at the right of the waiting room being used as a ladies' waiting room and toilet; the office and waiting rooms were heated by fireplaces in the back wall of the building, but the ladies' room does not appear to have been heated. There were no doors or windows in the rear wall, but the two brick chimney stacks that rose from the above-mentioned fireplaces provided visual interest to this otherwise blank wall.

Other buildings at Appledore included the engine shed at the end of the line, two railway cottages, a water tower and a small signal box. The engine shed contained a water crane which was fed from the nearby water tower, and a coaling stage was strategically-situated beside the shed.

The railway cottages were sited at right angles to the platform with their gable end facing the track, and the signal cabin was situated on the platform to the north of the station building. The latter structure was, in reality, little more than a single storey lever cabin – its outward appearance being particularly undistinguished; it did, however, contain the frame controlling the station's up starting and down home signals, together with a subsidiary siding arm below the home signal that controlled entry to the yard.

Maps prepared in conjunction with Major J.W. Pringle's 1908 Board of Trade inspection furnish a tantalising glimpse of the signalling arrangements in force in 1908, and as the station was closed in 1917 these arrangements are unlikely to have been altered throughout the station's brief life. In view of the general paucity of information on Bideford, Westward Ho! &

Station master Harold Moody stands on the platform at Appledore, while the engine of an incoming train runs-round the single coach. *Collection of D.J. Powell*

Appledore station after closure and demolition. When photographed by Mr Kidner in May 1936, the trackbed had been converted into a road, though the platform (*right*) and store (*left*) remained in place. *R.W. Kidner*

Appledore signalling, it will be of interest to summarise the details contained in the 1908 BoT report.[32]

Appledore signal box contained a 10-lever frame* with nine working levers and one white-painted 'spare'. Levers 8, 9, and probably also No. 1 were signal levers, while numbers 3, 5 and 7 worked the run-round loop and siding points. Levers 2, 4 and 6 were intended to work ground discs, though a pencilled comment appended to the signalling diagram prepared for Major Pringle suggests that the requirement for ground discs had been 'waived' at an early date. There is, for this reason, a question mark over the ground discs listed below, though, on the assumption that they were – at least initially – provided, it would seem that the lever frame at Appledore station was arranged as follows:

Signal or turnout	Lever No.	Probable Colour
Up main home signal	No. 1	Red
Run-round loop entry ground disc	No. 2	Red
Main to run-round loop up facing points	No. 3	Black
Siding to loop ground disc	No. 4	Red
Siding to loop points	No. 5	Black
Run-round loop exit (up) ground disc	No. 6	Red
Main to run-round down facing points	No. 7	Black
Down main home siding arm	No. 8	Red
Down main home signal	No. 9	Red
Spare lever	No. 10	White

The colours shown above are conjectural, but as most Edwardian railway companies painted their signal levers red and point levers black these same colours are likely to have been employed on the Bideford, Westward Ho! & Appledore line. The one element of doubt, in this context, concerns the up and down signal levers; some companies distinguished their up and down levers by painting them in different colours, red being a favourite colour for up signals while blue was often employed to denote down signal levers. This system (or something similar) may have been adopted on the BWH&AR line, but in the absence of firm information it seems reasonable to suggest that the company would have painted its signal levers in the usual red, white and black colours.

Appledore had one incongruous feature in that it was the only station on the Bideford, Westward Ho! & Appledore line to boast a footbridge; this structure carried a footpath from Irsha Street to nearby allotment gardens.

Appledore station was lit by gas, and the platform was well-equipped with weighing machines, timetable boards and platform seats. A low, stone-built wall extended along the rear of the platform, and this was topped by iron railings which were supported by raised brick pillars – the overall effect being particularly pleasing.

The question of goods traffic at Appledore has already been discussed, but it may be worth repeating that goods facilities are not shown in the Railway Clearing House *Handbook of Stations*. On the other hand, the siding at Appledore would clearly have been used for engineering purposes, and for bringing in supplies of locomotive coal. It was also one of the few 'spare' sidings available for stock storage on the Bideford, Westward Ho! &

---

* It is not known whether the facing points were fitted with facing point locks.

Appledore line, and for this reason it is likely that all or most of the railway's nine goods vehicles would have been parked there when they were not needed elsewhere on the line. (Bideford Town Council did not like railway vehicles being parked on the quay siding, and bearing in mind the lack of goods sidings at Bideford Yard, it is hard to see where else the BWH&AR wagons could have been parked when they were not in use!)

Appledore was of course one of the few properly staffed stations on the BWH&AR and the fact that two railway cottages were provided suggests that at least two railway families lived here. The locally-based staff may have been permanent way men or train crews, while there may also have been a requirement for porter-signalmen or other general purpose platform staff; such men would have been needed to work the points and signalling, carry passengers' luggage and deal with occasional small parcels or merchandise traffic.

Appledore's station master was Mr Harold Robert Moody, who had previously been the proprietor of The Rising Sun Inn in Irsha Street. Like his colleague John Loughlin at Westward Ho!, Mr Moody seems to have combined his duties on the Bideford, Westward Ho! & Appledore Railway with other interests, and in this context it is interesting to find that, according to the 1910 *Kelly's Directory of Devon*, he was both station master and proprietor of a 'Public Hall'. The Public Hall in question was probably the one in Irsha Street that had featured in the Opening Day celebrations on 1st May, 1908.

Victorian and Edwardian railway stations were often liberally-supplied with huts, sheds and stores, but this does not appear to have been the case on the Bideford, Westward Ho! & Appledore line. Lamp rooms, bicycle sheds and permanent way huts were few and far between on the BWH&AR route, and although such buildings *must* have been needed, there were virtually none of these ancillary structures at the main stations. It is likely that, at Appledore, a small mess room would have been provided for the benefit of locomotive crews, but otherwise the only minor building at the terminus was a sort of store or lock-up beside the siding. This building, which was solidly-built of local stone, had a sliding door that opened directly onto the track so that loading or unloading could take place; it may have been a goods shed, but in view of the paucity of goods facilities elsewhere on the BWH&AR line, it is perhaps more likely that the building functioned as a store for locomotive coal or permanent way materials.

Appledore station was well-sited in relation to nearby shops and houses, and having arrived at this North Devon seaport by train, Edwardian travellers were only a few steps away from the 'town centre'.

In many ways an archetypal West Country seaport, Appledore was an attractive coastal town, filled with narrow alleyways and quaint old buildings. Boat yards and slipways lined the waterfront, while vessels were able to come alongside for loading or unloading at the New Quay. Some of the neighbouring dry docks were able to accommodate three-masted barques or other large vessels, but the most characteristic sailing craft used in the area during the early 1900s were ketches and schooners – some of which had actually been built on the Torridge.

Vessels seen at Appledore during the Edwardian period included the ketches *Swan* and *Irene*, the barquentine *Belle of the Exe*, and the schooners *Rose*, *Katie*, *Juniper* and *Annie Reece*. A few years later, in 1927, the 74-gun wooden battleship HMS *Revenge* – a veteran of Trafalgar – came to Appledore for breaking up; by that time, however, the Bideford, Westward Ho! & Appledore Railway was no more.

A c.1935 aerial view of Appledore. The station was sited on the far side of the settlement, near the parish church. *Oakwood Collection*

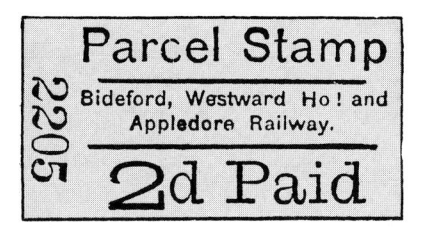

Parcel Stamp
2205
Bideford, Westward Ho! and Appledore Railway.
2d Paid

A busy scene at Westward Ho! station. An up train is obviously due, though the crossing gates have not yet been opened. The brick-built station building was smaller than that at Appledore; it contained toilet and waiting room facilities. Note the absence of a down starting signal – though the up home can be clearly seen beyond the level crossing.

Rob Dark Collection

Chapter Six
Subsequent History and Minor Details

The Bideford, Westward Ho! & Appledore Railway eked out a somewhat impecunious existence throughout the Edwardian period. Although owned by the British Electric Traction Company this isolated seven mile line retained many of the attributes of an independent concern, and most ordinary travellers would probably have been blissfully unaware that the BWH&AR was part of the BET empire!

The line soon became an accepted part of the local scene, and in spite of the earlier problems with Bideford Town Council, there is at least some evidence to suggest that local people learned to view the railway – and particularly the street tramway section – as a minor tourist attraction. The line became a favourite subject among local photographers, and most Edwardian postcard views of Bideford Quay managed to depict at BWH&AR train on this attractive, tree-lined boulevard.

In summer time the line carried large numbers of local people in addition to its usual quota of summer visitors, and many children were taken along the line to Cornborough or Westward Ho! as a Sunday School 'Treat'. On market days, the railway carried country people to and from Bideford, while special trains continued to be arranged in connection with dances or other special events.

Two Contrasting Glimpses

Guide book writers were interested in the railway both as a means of transport and as a local peculiarity, and the following extract from one of the 'Homeland' series of guide books provides a useful glimpse of the railway as it appeared to contemporary eyes:

> It is not always easy to give praise to a railway, but the Bideford, Westward Ho! & Appledore Railway, in spite of its high-sounding title, is singularly modest and unobtrusive. To be sure it is well in evidence at Westward Ho! having a station on the front, but elsewhere it comes as a surprise to the walker along the lanes around Abbotsham and Kenwith.
>
> It is well worth taking the full trip of half-an-hour's duration if only for the sake of the scenery, which changes as rapidly as it unfolds; now, as Appledore is left, the broad expanse of the golf links, now a burst of tumultuous sea as the train takes the sharp bend past Westward Ho!. Now a tunnelling amid deep tree shadows at Abbotsham and Kenwith, through the marshy meadow land behind Bideford, and finally the pleasant Torridge on our left as we run on to the quay by Kingsley's statue.
>
> The line is some seven miles long, with termini at Bideford and Appledore. There is a suggestion of primitiveness about the curious little engine, boxed in as it is down to the rails in order that dogs and cattle may not attempt suicide by running beneath.
>
> Halts are provided in addition to the principal stations, and armed with a timetable the pedestrian will often find it possible to make a swift and agreeable termination to his walk.[33]

Dudley Clark, the author of this extract, evidently saw the BWH&AR as an asset for walkers and other tourists, but Charles C. Harper, who also knew the railway in its operational days, was less appreciative. In his book *The North Devon Coast* (1908), Mr Harper referred in incredulous terms, to 'the weird-looking engine' that he found standing in the middle of a public highway:

> The rails run onto the roadway, and end without the formality of a station, platforms, signals or anything of the kind. And the weird-looking engine, when it goes dragging the one or two carriages after it, glides away with the air of tomorrow being plenty of time to do the work of today.

Having made fun of the BWH&AR 2–4–2Ts, and their compulsory 4 mph crawl through Bideford's streets, the author settled down to savour the pastoral scenery of the Kenwith Valley. Unfortunately, he then arrived at Westward Ho!. As intimated in Chapter Five, Westward Ho! was never really completed, and although a seaside resort was created beside Pebble Ridge, it stubbornly refused to develop along the lines of conventional resorts such as Ilfracombe or Torquay. This fact was gleefully noted by Mr Harper, who described the place as 'a sad collection of forlorn houses, dressed in penitential grey plaster' and occupying an area of 'flat lands and sandy wastes' beside the sea. 'Three fourths of the houses' were empty, continued Mr Harper, while the others were 'chiefly occupied by people who wonder why they ever came – and wish they hadn't'.

A Failed Resort?

It is possible that Mr Harper visited Westward Ho! on a wet winter's day – in which case three quarters of the houses probably *would* have been empty. However, if we discount the element of exaggeration in his description of the resort, the author of *The North Devon Coast* was entirely correct in his assessment of Westward Ho!. This artificially-created seaside holiday centre was, in many ways, a failure. Streets were laid out but never finished, large hotels were built but never filled by paying guests, and – most damning of all – holidaymakers never travelled to the resort in large numbers during the Victorian or Edwardian periods.

Westward Ho! remained a small scale resort throughout the 19th and early 20th centuries. In 1901, for example, its population was only 693, while in 1911 this meagre total had dropped still further to 655. Whatever criteria one applies Westward Ho! was a failure in terms of large scale resort development, and this, in turn, guaranteed that the Bideford, Westward Ho! & Appledore Railway would similarly fail to develop as its promoters had originally intended.

If the railway had been connected to the main line system there might have been a happier outcome to the story of Westward Ho!. As Charles Harper perceptively noted, the promoters of the little resort over-looked the fact that Westward Ho! 'was on the way to nowhither ... and there consequently never could be, by any chance, an easy and convenient approach from any large town whence holidaymakers come'.[34]

It was, by 1913, clear to all concerned that the Bideford, Westward Ho! & Appledore Railway would never be a money-spinner, and although the BET Company continued to operate the line, the BWH&AR remained little more than an obscure and isolated branch line.

Proposed Petrol Railcar Operation

In an attempt to operate the railway on a more cost-efficient basis the line's owners considered the introduction of petrol-engined railcars. Such vehicles would have enabled the BWH&AR to operate as a tramway without the additional cost of electrification, and in this sense one can understand the attractions of railcar operation on the Westward Ho! line.

In 1913 Henry Sowden, the BWH&AR General Manager, wrote to the Board of Trade as he was obliged to do under the terms of the 1896 Act of Parliament in relation to changes of motive power on 'Railway or Tramway Number One'. With his letter, he enclosed plans of a 60 horse power Leyland petrol-engined vehicle which the Bideford, Westward Ho! & Appledore Directors wished to employ on the Westward Ho! line. The vehicle depicted was not unlike a conventional four-wheeled tramcar; it could be driven from either end, and passengers were accommodated in a single saloon. The vehicle weighed 12 tons, and it was lit by acetylene gas.[35]

The proposed petrol-driven railcar was similar, in most respects, to the Leyland petrol trams that had been introduced by the Morecambe Tramway Company in 1912. However, as Mr Sowden pointed out in his letter to the Board of Trade, the proposed BWH&AR vehicle was an improved version of the Morecambe cars, having a more powerful engine (60 hp as opposed to 55 hp) and a heavier weight of 12 tons.

The Board of Trade was willing to approve the proposed petrol railcar for use on Railway or Tramway Number One subject to additional precautions in respect of the petrol tanks, but sadly, World War I intervened before the railcar idea could be put into effect.

Boardroom Changes

The composition of the Bideford, Westward Ho! & Appledore Board had undergone several changes since the formation of the BWH&AR Company, as an independent concern, back in 1896. Of the original three Directors, George Taylor and Charles Eagle Bott had left the Board by the turn-of-the-century, and only Captain Molesworth then remained.

The Bideford, Westward Ho! & Appledore Directors in 1903 were as follows:

Name	Address
F.W. Chanter (Chairman)	Frethey, Taunton, Somerset
Captain George Frederick Molesworth, RN	Torridge House, Westward Ho!, Devon
H.S. Day	Donington House, Norfolk Street, London
C.L. Robertson	Donington House, Norfolk Street, London

It will be noted that Mr Day and Mr Robertson apparently shared the same address, but this apparent mystery is resolved when one discovers that 'Donington House', Norfolk Street, The Strand, London WC was the head office of the British Electric Traction Company. Both of these Directors were BET representatives on the BWH&AR Board, while Mr Chanter, the BWH&AR Chairman was the British Electric Traction Company's representative in Western England.

The Bideford, Westward Ho! & Appledore Railway General Manager in 1903 was Henry Sowden, while engineering responsibilities were shared by Stephen Sellon, the BET Chief Engineer, and Mr W.J. Gale, who had acted as Resident Engineer during the construction of the Bideford to Northam line.

Ten years later, in 1913, the BWH&AR Directors included Charles H. Dade (Chairman), H.S. Day, and the redoubtable Captain Molesworth – who continued to represent local interests on the Board. Mr Day and Mr Dade were both BET representatives and their address was given as 1, Kingsway, London WC. The General Manager at this time was still Henry Sowden who, like Captain Molesworth, had been associated with the BWH&AR line from its inception.

While on the subject of Bideford, Westward Ho! & Appledore Directors, it is of interest to note that Captain George F. Molesworth appears to have lived a sort of itinerant existence within the general area of Westward Ho!. In 1902, for instance, he was apparently living in some style at Torridge House, Westward Ho! whereas by 1906 he had moved to a new property known as 'The Chalet'. The latter building was situated within yards of Westward Ho! station, and in this context one must inevitably ask how station master John Loughlin would have felt about having a Director and Founding Father of the railway company on his very doorstep! Amusingly, Captain Molesworth's next change of address took him even closer to Mr Loughlin, in that he moved into No. 2 Nelson Terrace – actually next door to the station master who occupied Nos. 3 and 4![36]

Captain Molesworth was still residing at 2, Nelson Terrace in 1910 – by which time station master Loughlin had himself moved to 'Camden'. There is an element of comedy in these frequent changes of residence, and one cannot help noticing that Mr Loughlin had moved 'up-market' while Captain Molesworth was descending inexorably 'down-market' from detached villa to Victorian terraced house!

The 1913 *Kelly's Directory of Devon* reveals that Captain Molesworth was, by that time, giving his address as 'The Union Club, Westward Ho!' this being his fourth change of address in 11 years. In reality, this former naval officer probably lived in a succession of lodgings – perhaps because (like many ex-sailors) he simply could not settle on dry land.

There is a very real suspicion that the Captain's personal wealth was slowly being eroded through his involvement with the railway and with failed property ventures in and around Westward Ho!. Falling income would explain his frequent changes of address, but at the same time one can only admire the tenacity with which Captain George F. Molesworth maintained his benevolent interest in the Bideford, Westward Ho! & Appledore Railway; he also showed a remarkable attachment to Westward Ho! and in contrast to many property speculators (failed or otherwise) he had no hesitation in actually living amid the new residential developments that he had himself helped to create.

World War I

It is generally accepted that the years from 1900 until 1914 constituted the 'Golden Age' of British railways. In those settled years before World War I the railways, great and small, enjoyed an undisputed monopoly of land transport, and with motor transport little more than an unpleasant cloud on the horizon, obscure lines such as the BWH&AR route could survive on the basis that they offered much-needed local transport facilities.

The outbreak of World War I in August 1914 brought the Golden Age of rail transport to a sudden and brutal close, and in the next few years the various British railway systems struggled to maintain their services against a background of rising costs and labour shortages. Railwaymen were, in theory, exempt from conscription when that measure was introduced in 1916, but many railway employees were members of the reserve forces and, as such, they were among the very first men to see active service; many more railwaymen volunteered, with the result that lines such as the Westward Ho! route were obliged to employ men who would otherwise have retired.

Although Bideford was far from the Western Front, the BWH&AR line played a small, but active part during the early days of the war when it conveyed naval reservists from Appledore to Bideford on the first stage of their journey to join the Fleet in August 1914. Later, the railway gained at least some extra wartime traffic when a Royal Naval Air Station was established at Westward Ho!.

The exigencies of wartime operation led to some minor curtailments and adjustments in train services, one of the most significant alterations put into effect at this time being the cancellation of the early-morning down service from Bideford to Appledore. There had, for several years, been a down service from Bideford at 7.50 am, and this first down train later formed the 8.25 am up working from Appledore. By September 1915, however, the first up train of the day was still leaving Appledore at the time-honoured time of 8.25 am, but with no early morning down train from Bideford it became necessary to out-station one of the engines at Appledore overnight in order to work the revised timetable.

The September 1915 timetable provided 10 up and 10 down trains, with up services from Appledore to Bideford at 8.25, 9.45, 11.25 am, 12.35, 1.45, 2.55, 4.17, 5.30, 6.40 and 8.15 pm. In the reverse direction, balancing down workings left Bideford Quay at 9.10, 10.50 am, 12.00, 1.10, 2.20, 3.30, 4.52, 6.05, 7.40 and 9.15 pm respectively.

Closure and Requisition

In 1916 the government decided that locomotives, rails and other railway equipment was needed for military purposes in France and elsewhere, and in order to fulfil this requirement a number of minor railways were earmarked for closure and requisitioning. One of these lines was the Bideford, Westward Ho! & Appledore route which, being far from centres of major industry or population, was seen as an ideal candidate for military use.

The last trains ran in March 1917, and after hurried preparations for their departure, the three BWH&AR 2-4-2Ts were moved across Bideford Bridge to the LSWR station at East-the-Water on Sunday 29th March, 1917. To facilitate this operation, temporary trackwork was laid from the end of the line at Bideford Quay and thence westwards for a short distance into Bridge

One of the three locomotives (probably *Torridge*) makes its way across Bideford Bridge *en route* for the LSWR goods yard and the journey to France.
Oakwood Collection

A BWH&AR engine inches its way along temporary tracks as it proceeds through the narrow streets of Bideford. *Oakwood Collection*

Street. From there, a turnout provided a means of access to the bridge – a reverse shunt being necessary before the engines could cross the river.

Hundreds of people lined the narrow streets of Bideford as, one by one, the engines slowly made their way along the temporary track. For some onlookers, the departure of the locomotives was viewed with mixed emotions – there were, after all, people in Bideford who had never liked the railway in the first place; others, perhaps even the majority, were sad to see the 2–4–2Ts leave Bideford. Later, in the evening, the gangers who had laid the temporary rails joined some of the townsfolk in an impromptu wake, and several local people, overcome with emotion (and alcohol) were arrested for drinking out of hours!

On Monday 30th March, the three engines were moved through the streets of Bideford East-the-Water to the London & South Western Railway goods yard, and having finally reached the main line system, they were able to proceed to a locomotive works for overhaul prior to being sent overseas.

Lost at Sea?

At this point, Bideford, Westward Ho! & Appledore history enters into the realm of myth and legend. It is said that two, or perhaps even all three of the BWH&AR engines were subsequently loaded aboard a steamer at Avonmouth, from where they set out on a circuitous voyage to France via the Bristol Channel, Lands End and the English Channel. This voyage is said to have taken place aboard the screw steamer *Götterdammerung*, which, sadly, was torpedoed by a U-boat off the Cornish coast near Padstow.[37]

Needless to say, this story has many inconsistencies. If the engines were being sent to France, why were they shipped from Avonmouth and not one of the Channel ports? And how could a vessel with the name *Götterdammerung* have retained its blatantly Germanic name at a time when 'anti-Hun' sentiments were running at fever pitch?

Leaving these questions for the moment, it is interesting to note that tales of a British transport being sunk in the English Channel while loaded with railway equipment are strangely persistent. Track and other material lifted from the Great Western Railway's Uxbridge High Street branch, for example, is supposed to have been lost on a torpedoed ship in the early months of 1917, while a similar fate is said to have met the Caledonian Railway's Inchture tramway, which had been requisitioned for military use in January 1916.

Bideford, Uxbridge and Inchture are widely-scattered places at opposite ends of the country, yet stories of railway equipment being shipped off to France in 1917 and lost *en route* to the front are told in each of these places. There is thus some corroborative evidence to support the story of a sinking in the period March to April 1917; there is, moreover, no doubt that enemy U-boats were particularly active at that time, not only in the North Atlantic but also around the coasts of the United Kingdom. Allied shipping losses went up from 386,000 tons in January 1917 to an unprecedented total of 881,000 tons in April, while in that same year German U-boats made at least 250 recorded passages through the supposedly well-defended English Channel.

These worrying facts, though well-known to the government, were withheld from the public, and with strict censorship in force it is quite possible that valuable equipment *could* have been lost on the way to France. There may even have been some major disaster – some spectacular German success within sight of the British coast – that warranted special secrecy, and it may be that this catastrophe has remained an Official Secret to this very day.

Whatever happened on that fateful voyage in 1917, the fact remains that at least two BWH&AR locomotives simply disappeared from the records – though it is known that *Kingsley* was subsequently sold to the National Smelting Company, and was finally scrapped in 1937.[38]

Two other facts should also be noted; firstly, Lloyd's List would seem to suggest that the screw-steamer *Götterdammerung* never existed (at least not in 1917) and secondly, divers have recently located a wrecked steamer off the coast of Padstow. This vessel is said to have been carrying railway engines at the time of its demise, and at the time of writing there are suggestions that these engines are, in fact, the two lost 2–4–2Ts *Torridge* and *Grenville*.

Post-Closure Developments

It was by no means certain, in 1917, that the Westward Ho! line would not re-open after the war. In the event, the changed conditions pertaining after World War I made it unlikely that the line would ever be revived, and although the BWH&AR passenger vehicles remained locked in their shed at Bideford for several years, it soon became clear that the Bideford, Westward Ho! & Appledore Railway was well and truly defunct. The introduction of rural 'bus services ensured that the transport needs of Appledore and Westward Ho! could still be served, and in the next few years a company known as 'Royal Motor Services' maintained a useful road link between Bideford, Westward Ho! and Appledore

Interestingly, the Bideford, Westward Ho! & Appledore route continued to feature in *Bradshaw's Timetables*, but closer examination of the BWH&AR table revealed that the service advertised was in fact the Royal Motor 'bus route. In later years, the Westward Ho! service became a Southern National route, and Westward Ho! station survived for many years as a Southern National 'bus station.

The BWH&AR coaches were finally auctioned at Bideford by R. Blackmore & Sons in April 1921, and most of them were sent to the Midlands for disposal. One vehicle was conveyed to Westward Ho! for further use as a beach hut on the sand hills to the west of the former station, while in May 1925 *The Railway Magazine* reported that 'several old coaches, which apparently belonged at one time to the Bideford, Westward Ho! & Appledore Railway' could be seen 'utilised for dwelling purposes at Wellingborough, near the LNWR station'.

The abandoned railway was gradually converted into roads and footpaths, an important development in this respect being the construction of Kingsley Road along part of the trackbed at the Bideford end of the line. This work was carried out in the 1920s at a cost of £27,000, while, in a subsequent

Westward Ho! station found a new role as a bus station, its platforms remaining in use while the signal cabin was enlarged to form a cafe and snack bar.
D.J. Powell Collection

In this 1964 view, a bus stands alongside the former station building. Station Hall (*right*) remained in use for public entertainments. *D.J. Powell Collection*

railway-to-road conversion, Torridge Road was built along the alignment of the former line between Appledore station and Richmond Road Halt. By a happy coincidence, these new road schemes employed the names 'Torridge' and 'Kingsley', thereby commemorating two of the three BWH&AR locomotives!

In February 1937 Mr F. Wilkey, the Chairman of the Northam Urban District Council, suggested that the highly scenic coastal section of the abandoned railway might be turned into 'one of the finest marine drives in the country', and this proposal evoked a favourable response in many quarters. It was further suggested that the new coastal drive could be called 'Kipling Road' as a reminder of Rudyard Kipling's associations with the Westward Ho! area.[39]

Motoring was, in the 1930s, still a comparatively small scale affair, and at a time when roads were not yet choked with noisy, smelly motor vehicles, one can appreciate the attractions of a coastal 'drive' between Westward Ho! and Cornborough. In the event, the coastal drive was never made, and instead the most spectacular section of the Bideford, Westward Ho! & Appledore route became part of the Somerset and North Devon Coastal Path – an amenity for walkers and lovers of the countryside rather than a strip of tarmac for motorists and 'speed merchants'!

The coastal path idea originated in the late 1940s, but it took many years of planning and negotiations with landowners before this excellent idea could be brought to fruition. However, on 20th May, 1978, the Somerset & North Devon Coastal Footpath was finally opened by Denis Howell, the then Minister of State for the Environment, and a sizeable length of the former railway was thereby incorporated into one of Britain's finest long distance footpaths.

There had, meanwhile, been many changes elsewhere on the former BWH&AR line. At Appledore, for example, the station building was partially demolished, leaving the platform and rear wall of the station *in situ* beside Torridge Road, while Westward Ho! station remained more or less unaltered in its new role as a bus station. The low passenger platforms were ideal for use in conjunction with motor buses, and the waiting room and other buildings remained intact – the signal box becoming a café, while 'Station Hall' continued to be used for dances and other social functions.

At Bideford Yard, the substantially-built locomotive and carriage sheds were ideal for industrial or commercial use, and the spacious carriage shed soon found new employment as a garage and warehouse, while the engine shed was adapted for use as a dairy. After serving for a time as a bus garage, the carriage shed was later used by Messrs J.U. Fulford & Sons Ltd, a firm of agricultural merchants.

Having described the history of the Westward Ho! line until closure, and recounted some of the post-closure developments, it would be useful to add a few more details concerning trackwork, staffing and other matters that have not yet been fully explored.

The site of an abandoned level crossing near Abbotsham Road on 31st May, 1936. The stone-built hut originally housed a gate-keeper, though it may later have been used as a Permanent Way store. *R.W. Kidner*

Another glimpse of the former BWH&AR line in May 1936; the photograph was taken near Cornborough Cliffs. *R.W. Kidner*

Further Notes on Trackwork

The Bideford, Westward Ho! & Appledore Railway was laid with a variety of trackwork. The street tramway section in Bideford employed ordinary railway lines because tram lines would have been unsuitable for railway vehicles to run on – the sections and tolerances of railway and tram wheels being essentially different (tramway vehicles having shallower flanges than railway rolling stock).

As far as can be ascertained, the street tramway section was laid with 60 lb. per yard flat-bottomed steel rail resting on longitudinal wooden sleepers. The rails and sleepers were laid below the actual road surface so that the tops of the rails were flush with the roadway, and as previously explained, Jarrah wood blocks were used to pave the area between the rails, and a foot or two on either side.

It is unclear how the necessary groove was arranged, but photographic evidence suggests that two sets of rails may have been employed to form each groove; one rail appears to have been laid upright on the wooden sleepers while the other (inner) rail was laid on its side to form the required aperture (this procedure would not, of course have been necessary if the company had been able to use proper tram rails, which had a ready-made groove in their upper surfaces).

Details of the ordinary railway section between Bideford and Appledore have already been given, suffice to say the Bideford to Northam section was laid with 60 lb. per yard flat-bottomed rail, while the Northam to Appledore section was laid with 80 lb. per yard double-headed rail throughout most of its length; at Appledore station, however, lighter section (probably 60 lb.) flat-bottomed rail was employed, and it is possible that this permanent way material had been removed from Northam station. The line was ballasted with broken stone ballast which, in places, covered the sleepers.

Staff and Staff Numbers

Light railways were, by their very nature, cheaply constructed railways that dispensed with all or most of the non-vital aspects of railway operation. Unstaffed stations, open level crossings and simplified signalling were all intended to reduce labour and other costs, and for this reason lines such as the BWH&AR route employed fewer men than a normal Edwardian railway. Having said that, it comes as a surprise to discover that the Westward Ho! line needed a labour force of 25 or 26 people to keep it in operation.

When first opened, the original line from Bideford to Northam required a number of gate keepers at the various level crossings *en route* to Northam. Many of these employees were redeployed or made redundant in 1905, but there was still a requirement for gate keepers at the Chanter's Lane and Causeway crossings, together with at least four signalmen to man the boxes at Bideford Yard, Abbotsham Road, Westward Ho! and Northam (in 1908 the Northam signalman was presumably moved to Appledore).

Three locomotives would have needed two, and probably three sets of engine crews, while there would clearly have been a similar number of conductor-guards, necessitating (at the very least) six men actually to work

SUBSEQUENT HISTORY AND MINOR DETAILS 131

the trains. Additionally, there were station masters at Westward Ho! and Appledore, a General Manager at Bideford and at least one clerk at Bideford, a refreshment room manager at Westward Ho! and an indeterminate number of permanent way men, porters and labourers.

There was at least one inspector, this position being filled, around 1913, by Mr G. Kemp – who had joined the BWH&AR as a conductor in 1902 and manned the first train into Appledore in 1908. Mr Kemp and other BWH&AR employees are mentioned by name in the following list:

BWH&AR Employees During the Period 1912-1913

Name	Position	Nos.
Henry Sowden	General Manager, Bideford Quay	1
John Loughlin	Station master, Westward Ho!	1
Harold Robert Moody	Station master, Appledore	1
John Galliford	Refreshment room manager, Westward Ho!	1
G. Kemp	Inspector	1
F. Fursey	Gate/halt keeper, Causeway Crossing	1
–	Conductor guards	3(?)
–	Engine drivers	3(?)
–	Engine firemen	3(?)
–	Senior clerk (Appledore?)	1(?)
–	Junior clerk (Bideford)	1
–	Gate keeper, Chanter's Lane Halt	1
–	Signalman, Abbotsham Road	1
–	Signalman, Bideford Yard	1
–	Porter-signalman, Westward Ho!	1
–	Porter-signalman, Appledore	1
–	Ganger	1
–	PW men and labourers	3(?)
	TOTAL employees (conjectural figure)	26

Study of the above table will reveal that no allowance has been made for shift work, but as the Westward Ho! line was only worked to full capacity during the summer period there are unlikely to have been any 'spare' signalmen. By analogy with other light railways, signalmen or other employees may have carried out painting or other maintenance duties during the winter months, while conductors or other staff may have been laid off during the winter period (conversely, seasonal staff could well have been hired to deal with the crowds during the July and August holiday season).

Bideford, Westward Ho! & Appledore Uniforms

Like other railway and tramway companies, the BWH&AR issued at least some of its men with uniforms or protective clothing, and surviving photographs show that these uniforms were fairly conventional – though there is more than a suggestion of informality in some of the Edwardian photographs.[40]

Station masters wore dark blue (or possibly black) trousers, waistcoats and jackets, together with peaked hats, while engine drivers and firemen were issued with loose-fitting overalls. Permanent way men, in contrast, wore ordinary shirts, jackets and waistcoats. Some of the conductors appear to have worn a 'uniform' of jacket and peaked cap, but study of the photographs shown in this book will show that the majority of BWH&AR men apparently wore a mix of uniforms and ordinary clothes. Many of the men appear to have worn cloth caps – this familiar working class headgear being favoured by conductors, drivers, and permanent way men alike.

There is little indication that metal buttons, trouser piping, cap badges or other uniform features were worn, and although most Bideford, Westward Ho! & Appledore men did indeed wear uniforms, those uniforms must have seemed plain in relation to other British Electric Traction-owned lines.

The Railway Today

Today, three-quarters of a century after the closure of the Westward Ho! line, the course of this long-abandoned railway can still be traced, and numerous traces of its existence can still be found.

At Bideford, the tram lines have entirely disappeared, but walkers can follow the route of the line along the quay. The railway began midway between High Street and Cooper Street, and then ran due north for a short distance before turning west across the reclaimed Pill; this end of the line has now been transformed into Kingsley Road, and it is possible to follow the road towards Chanters Lane and Causeway crossings.

At the Causeway, the crossing keeper's cottage has been extended to form a larger dwelling. Continuing due west, the trackbed now runs across open fields, and despite modern farming methods, the route survives as a series of disconnected paths and tracks. In places, former level crossing gateposts remain *in situ*, while cuttings, embankments and underline culverts serve as visible reminders of the lost railway.

The line through the Kenwith Valley crosses private land, and it is thus unsuitable for walking, but at Cornborough Cliffs the road becomes a public right of way, and it is possible to walk on (or beside) the line all the way to Westward Ho!. Passing through cuttings and along raised embankments, the present day walker is left in little doubt that he is now following a former railway line. To the right, Kipling Torrs are now owned by the National Trust, and with the sea close at hand on the left hand side of the trackbed, this part of the BWH&AR route remains as attractive today as it was in the days when *Kingsley*, *Torridge* or *Grenville* clattered along the line with their one or two-coach trains.

Westward Ho! is today a thriving, albeit informal seaside resort, replete with chalets, caravans and holiday camps. It is ironic that, in modern times, this Victorian resort has emerged as a popular centre for family holidays; however, the people who now come in considerable numbers to spend their summer holidays at Westward Ho! arrive in Devon by motor car – cheap motoring being the decisive factor in the growth of the resort since World War II.

Westward Ho! station is still used as a bus station, and part of the platform area is now fenced off to form a bus terminus. Until quite recently, the

The BWH&AR trackbed near Bideford, photographed in 1992. *Colin Judge*

The scene near Kenwith Castle Halt in 1992, looking towards the cutting. *Colin Judge*

An underbridge near Kenwith Castle Halt. *Colin Judge*

A present-day scene of the trackbed looking towards Kenwith Castle and Bideford.
Colin Judge

A set of ornate gates alongside the road at the entrance to Abbotsham Road station site, 1992.
Colin Judge

Seafield House, one of the large Victorian villas erected in and around Westward Ho!, undergoes restoration in 1992. The abandoned BWH&AR trackbed can be seen to the right. *Colin Judge*

A final look at Appledore station. The footpath passes along the former platform and through the now-demolished waiting room, toilets and ticket office (note the plaque on the wall, the text of which is recorded on the opposite page). *Colin Judge*

station had survived intact, and the buses were able to run along the wide trackbed, while passengers used the platforms for embarking and disembarking. All of the buildings were intact at that time, the signal box being used as a tea room and the station building having been converted into a bungalow; the Station Hall remained in use as a theatre and dance hall, just as it had been in BWH&AR days.

The writer, who first visited Westward Ho! in the mid-1970s, was fascinated by this largely-intact BWH&AR station – which had obviously changed very little since the demise of the railway back in 1917. Although buses, rather than trains, were then using the platforms, the place seemed to exude the character of the Bideford, Westward Ho! & Appledore Railway, and one felt that, here at least, the spirit of the little railway lived on in a transmuted form.

Sadly, the present-day arrangements at Westward Ho! station are rather different. Station Hall has now been transformed into a restaurant and 'beer garden', with a new façade that now impinges on the former platform area. The adjacent station building has, regrettably, been demolished.

Moving northwards, the cheaply-constructed Appledore extension has left fewer earthworks, but at Appledore itself the rear wall of the station building can still be seen (1992). By following Torridge Road from Richmond Road Halt towards Appledore one can walk or drive straight through the former railway terminus. The raised platform was, until recently, still in place, but, following road improvements, a normal kerb has now been installed and a grassy slope extends from road level to the rear of the erstwhile platform.

The most conspicuous features at Appledore station are the two fireplaces that can still be seen in the ruined rear wall. Nearby, the railway cottages are still intact, and the stone wall that formerly ran along the back of the platform is *in situ* beside the present day pavement.

A metal plaque is affixed to what was once the rear wall of the gentlemen's urinal, and this informs modern visitors that they are standing on the site of the Bideford, Westward Ho! & Appledore Railway. A brief (though erroneous) history of the line is also given and this reads as shown below:

> This plaque commemorates the Bideford, Westward Ho!, Northam & Appledore Railway, which terminated at this station platform. This railway between Bideford Quay and Westward Ho! was opened in August 1901 and extended to Appledore in 1907. The total length was 7 miles and the charge 1*d*. a mile. In 1917 the rails and rolling stock were requisitioned for the war effort and sent to France.

Notes to Text

Sources are, in many cases, cited in the text, but the following brief notes may be of interest to those seeking further information on the BWH&AR line.

1. *Campden's Britannia* (Gibson's edition).
2. See *The Dictionary of National Biography* for further details of Kingsley, Drake, Grenville, etc.
3. Quoted by Sabine Baring-Gould in *Devon* (1907), p. 235.
4. The full story of the Lynn & Hunstantion Railway can be found in *The Lynn & Hunstanton Railway* (1987) by S.C. Jenkins.
5. The *Journal of the House of Commons*, 16th July, 1866.
6. The Bideford line was worked by the contractor Thomas Brassey for several years, but when his lease expired in 1863 the LSWR assumed control, mixed gauge being laid so that standard gauge LSWR stock could work over the route.
7. The *Journal of the House of Commons*, 17–18th February, 1896.
8. *Ibid.* 21st May, 1896.
9. The *Journal of the House of Commons*, 1898 *passim*.
10. PRO MT6 files 1553.
11. The *Journal of the House of Commons*, 25th July, 1898.
12. The British Electric Traction Company had been formed in 1896, by Emile Garcke. Its capital was £2,000,000, and its stated aims included 'the development of electric traction in England'.
13. PRO MT6 files 1395/1.
14. PRO MT6 files 1395/1.
15. As there would seem to be some doubt regarding the correct opening date of the Westward Ho! line (some authorities quoting 24th April, 1901) it is worth noting that *The Railway Times* edition for Saturday 25th May, 1901, clearly states that the railway was 'opened on Monday last' (i.e. Monday 20th May, 1901).
16. PRO MT6 files 1395/1.
17. PRO MT6 files 1395/1.
18. PRO MT6 files 1001/1.
19. PRO MT6 files 1736/1.
20. PRO MT6 files 1395/1.
21. PRO MT6 files 1736/1.
22. PRO MT6 files 1736/1.
23. Station details were obtained from *Bradshaw's Timetables*, the Railway Clearing House *Handbook of Stations*, and 25-inch Ordnance Survey maps.
24. *Bradshaw's Timetables* 1902–17 *passim*.
25. *The Locomotive Magazine.*
26. *Ibid.*
27. PRO MT6 files 1395/1.
28. *The Bideford Gazette*, 16th February, 1937.
29. Douglas Stuckey, *The Bideford, Westward Ho! & Appledore Railway* (1962).

30. Eric Delderfield, *The North Devon Story* (1952).
31. *The Bideford Gazette*, 16th February, 1937.
32. PRO MT6 files 1736/1.
33. Quoted in *The Railway Magazine*, June 1917.
34. Charles C. Harper, *The North Devon Coast* (1908).
35. PRO MT6 files 2212/2.
36. *Kelly's Directory of Devon*, 1902–14.
37. Douglas Stuckey, *The Bideford, Westward Ho! & Appledore Railway* (1962).
38. *Ibid*.
39. *The Bideford Gazette*, 16th February, 1937.
40. In 1906 the BWH&AR spent £6 7s. 6d. on clothing for its employees.

Sources and Acknowledgments

Material for *The Bideford, Westward Ho! & Appledore* was obtained from a variety of sources including Acts of Parliament, the 1904 Light Railway Order, *The Journal of the House of Commons*, *The Journal of the House of Lords*, *Bradshaw's Shareholders' Manual*, *Bradshaw's Timetables*, *The Railway Times*, *Kelly's Directories of Devon*, *The Locomotive Magazine*, *The Railway Engineer*, *The Bideford Gazette* and *The North Devon Journal*. Most of this material was found in the University of Leicester library, and thanks are due to all those library staff who helped with this project.

Other important sources of evidence were found in the Public Record Office at Kew. These did, to some extent, duplicate the sources available at the University of Leicester, though some important items – notably the Board of Trade reports – can, of course, be found only at Kew.

The most important and useful Board of Trade records consulted for this study were as follows:

MT6 1395/1	BWH&AR general developments 1903–1905 and BoT inspection reports.
MT6 1553	BWH&AR preliminary details, etc. and general developments 1896–1907.
MT6 1934/4	Return of deposit.
MT6 1736/1	Preliminary details etc., and inspection of Appledore extension.
MT6 2212/2	Proposed introduction of petrol-engined railcar on BWH&AR.
MT6 1443/5	Proposed extension to Hartland, etc.
MT6 2199/1	Proposed extensions to Clovelly, etc.
MT6 1001/3	Formal abandonment of the Bideford & Clovelly Railway scheme.
MT6 2424/15	Government compensation (1914–18 war).
MT6 1837/2	Abandonment of certain lines.
ZPER 11/19	Press report of opening celebrations.

Appendix One
Chronological Survey of Important Dates and Developments

1838 Taw Vale Railway formed to build line from Exeter to Fremington.
1845 Exeter & Crediton Railway formed to build line from Exeter & Crediton.
1848 Line opened from Fremington to Barnstaple.
1851 Exeter & Crediton Railway opened to traffic (12th May).
1854 Taw Vale Railway changes its name to North Devon Railway (24th July).
North Devon Railway opened throughout to Barnstaple (1st August).
1855 Publication of Charles Kingsley's novel *Westward Ho!*.
Opening of Bideford Extension Railway from Barnstaple to Bideford.
1863 First houses built at Westward Ho! by a property company.
1865 Torrington Extension Railway obtains Act (19th June).
1866 Bideford, Appledore & Westward Ho! Railway obtained its Act (16th July).
1872 Bideford to Torrington line opened to traffic, but Bideford, Appledore & Westward Ho! scheme unable to proceed.
1896 Incorporation of Bideford, Westward Ho! & Appledore Railway (21st May).
Light Railways Act receives Royal Assent (14th August).
1897 Proposed Western Counties Electric Railways & Tramways Company.
1898 Incorporation of Bideford & Clovelly Railway (25th July).
Work begins on the Bideford, Westward Ho! & Appledore line.
1900 Bideford, Westward Ho! & Appledore locomotives erected at Leeds. First BWH&AR coaches arrive in Bideford.
1901 Ceremonial opening of the BWH&AR line (24th April).
Board of Trade inspection of Bideford to Northam line (14th May).
Opening of Bideford to Northam line (20th May).
BWH&AR prosecuted by local council for running train on the quay.
Clovelly scheme formally abandoned.
1902 Run-round loop laid on Bideford Quay leads to dispute with Borough Council.
1903 Railway re-inspected by Board of Trade Inspector (26th March).
Station Hall opened for concerts, etc., at Westward Ho!.
1904 Light Railway Order obtained for Bideford loop line and Appledore extension.
Bideford run-round loop 'passed' by Board of Trade (17th December).
1905 Most level crossing gates removed as light railway procedures introduced.
1908 Appledore extension inspected by Board of Trade Inspector (23rd April).
Appledore extension opened for public traffic (1st May).
1913 Proposed petrol railcar.
1914 Start of World War I (August).
1917 Locomotives requisitioned for war service and BWH&AR closed (March).
1921 BWH&AR coaches auctioned at Bideford (April).
1928 Kingsley Road constructed along track at Bideford.
1937 Proposed 'Marine Drive' for motor vehicles from Bideford to Westward Ho!.
1978 Coastal section of BWH&AR route incorporated into the Somerset & North Devon Coast Path (20th May).

Appendix Two
Facilities at Bideford, Appledore and Intermediate Stations

BIDEFORD QUAY
Run-round loop
Goods siding (approximately six chains in length)
Booking office and waiting room in premises at 20, The Quay

BIDEFORD STRAND ROAD HALT
No facilities

BIDEFORD YARD
Six chain passing loop
14-lever signal cabin
Two-road carriage shed
Two-road locomotive shed
Coal store
Office and mess rooms
Up and down signals

CHANTERS LANE
Level crossing
Up and down signals
Gate keeper's lodge

CAUSEWAY CROSSING HALT
Level crossing
Up and down signals
Raised (two and a half storey) signal cabin
Crossing/halt keeper's dwelling
Passenger platform on down side (approximately 30 ft long × 6 in. high)

KENWITH CASTLE HALT
Level crossing (gates removed 1905)

ABBOTSHAM ROAD STATION
Crossing loop (approximately 5.75 chains in length)
Up and down passenger platforms (both approximately 30 ft long × 6 in. high)
Signal cabin with eight levers
Level crossing (gates removed 1905)
Up and down signals

CORNBOROUGH CLIFFS HALT
Passenger platform on up side of line (approximately 30 ft long × 6 in. high)

WESTWARD HO! STATION
Crossing loop (approximately eight chains in length)
Up and down platforms, each 320 ft long and 1 ft above rail level
Goods siding serving Westward Ho! gas works (approximately 6½ chains long)
Waiting room and public toilet facilities (possibly also booking office)
Refreshment room and book stall
Signal cabin with eight levers
Two level crossings (one at each end of the platforms)
Level crossing ground frame with two levers
Siding ground frame (at gas works) with two levers
Station Hall for concerts and entertainments
Up and down signals

141

BEACH ROAD HALT
Level crossing, but no other facilities (crossing gates removed 1905)

NORTHAM STATION
180 ft passenger platform on down side of line
Waiting room and toilets
Level crossing (gates removed)
Loop and engine spur (removed 1908)
Signal cabin with five levers (closed 1908)

RICHMOND ROAD
Level crossing (no gates)
Passenger platform with waiting shed

LOVER'S LANE HALT
Passenger platform without shelter

APPLEDORE STATION
Passenger platform on down side of line, 300 ft long and 1 ft above rail level
Run-round loop and one dead-end siding
Waiting rooms, booking office and public toilet facilities
Signal cabin with ten levers
Engine shed
Pedestrian footbridge
Two railway cottages
Water tower
Coal store
Up and down signals

LOCOMOTIVE COAL AND WATERING FACILITIES
A hydrant or column was provided at Appledore, and similar facilities were probably available at Bideford Yard – either attached to a raised water tank or via a piped supply to hydrants within the locomotive shed.

Bibliography

The Bideford, Westward Ho! & Appledore Railway was an obscure line, but it was situated in a popular holiday area, and although little has been written on the BWH&AR itself there is no shortage of information in relation to Devonshire local history. The following list of published works includes both railway and local history titles, and it is hoped that these will be of use to readers seeking further information on the BWH&AR line.

Eric Delderfield	*The North Devon Story* (1952).
Douglas Stuckey	*The Bideford, Westward Ho! & Appledore Railway* (1962).
Julia & Jonathan Baxter	*The Bideford, Westward Ho! & Appledore Railway.*
Roger Kidner	The Bideford, Westward Ho! & Appledore Railway, *Locomotion*, September 1936, pps. 35–36.
	Minor Standard Gauge Railways (1981), pp. 9, 50.
Sabine Baring-Gould	*The Little Guide to Devon* (1907).
John Beara	*Appledore: Handmaid of the Sea* (1976).

W.H. Bett	Ticket Spotlight, *Railway World*, 1961, p. 404.
Charles Klapper	The Rise & Fall of the Light Railway, *Railway World*, July 1968.
Charles Kingsley	*Westward Ho!* (1855).
Rudyard Kipling	*Stalkey & Co.* (1899).
Charles G. Harper	*The North Devon Coast* (1908).
Clive Gunnell	*The Somerset & North Devon Coast Path* (1981).
Muriel Goaman	*Old Bideford & District* (1968).
Mary Gray	*The North Devon Coast* (1974).
S.H. Burton	*The North Devon Coast* (Werner Laurie) (1953).
W.J. Slade	*Out of Appledore.*
Frank E. Whiting	*The Long Bridge of Bideford Through the Centuries* (1945).

By the Same Author

The Witney & East Gloucestershire Railway (Oakwood Press, 1975).
The Oxford, Worcester & Wolverhampton Railway (Oakwood Press, 1977) co-author.
The Lakeside & Haverthwaite Railway (Dalesman Publishing Co., 1977) co-author.
The Great Western & Great Central Joint Railway (Oakwood Press, 1978).
Walk Round Witney (Witney & District Historical & Archaeological Society, 1979).
Branch Lines into the Eighties (David & Charles, 1980) co-author.
The Fairford Branch (Oakwood Press, 1985).
The Lynn & Hunstanton Railway (Oakwood Press, 1987).
The Woodstock Branch (Wild Swan Press, 1987).
The Wells-next-the-Sea Branch (Oakwood Press, 1988).
The Cromer Branch (Oakwood Press, 1989).
The Moretonhampstead & South Devon Railway (Oakwood Press, 1989) co-author.
The Northampton & Banbury Junction Railway (Oakwood Press, 1990).
The Watford to St Albans Branch (Oakwood Press, 1990).
The Alston Branch (Oakwood Press, 1991).
The Leek & Manifold Railway (Oakwood Press, 1991).
The Rothbury Branch (Oakwood Press, 1991).
The Melton Constable to Cromer Branch (Oakwood Press, 1991).
The Helston Branch Railway (Oakwood Press, 1992).
The Cork, Blackrock & Passage Railway (Oakwood Press, 1993).
The Lynn & Dereham Railway (Oakwood Press, 1993).
The Wensleydale Line (Oakwood Press, 1993).

A Note on the Author

Born in London, Stanley C. Jenkins has degrees from the University of Lancaster and the University of Leicester. After working as a teacher and lecturer for several years, he is now employed by English Heritage as the Regional Curator for South Western England.

Index

Appledore 12–4, 16–7, 26, 47, 50, 55–7, 61–3, 67, 77–8, 80, 110, 113–7, 128, 131, 137, 142
Abbotsham Road 29, 38, 44, 61–2, 77–8, 97–9, 126, 130, 141

Beach Road Halt 44, 62, 142
Bideford 1, 2, 4, 8–18, 20, 34–6, 41, 43–4, 46–51, 61, 65, 77–8, 80–9, 119, 128, 130, 132, 141
Bideford, Appledore & Westward Ho! Railway 16–8
Bideford, Westward Ho! & Appledore Railway
  Closure 123
  Construction 34–6, 55–57
  Opening 37–40, 57–8
  Origins of 20–33
Bott, Charles Eagle (Director) 27, 121
British Electric Traction Company 34, 36–7, 47, 50, 55, 119, 120, 121, 132

Causeway Crossing Halt 40, 42, 44, 51, 62–3, 78, 89–92, 94, 130, 132, 141
Chanter, F.W. (Director) 9, 121
Chanter's Lane Halt 32, 42, 44, 62, 78, 132, 141
Clovelly, extension to 29–30, 33–6, 47, 93
Cornborough Cliffs Halt 20, 38, 44, 62, 99–101, 119, 128–9, 132, 141

Dade, Charles H. (Director) 122
Day, H.S. (Director) 9, 121–2

Electrification, proposed 47, 55

Gale, W.J. (Engineer) 9
Goods traffic 44, 61–2, 76, 115
Great Western Railway 15, 71, 125
Grenville, Sir Richard 11–3

Hill, George (Bideford & Clovelly Director) 33
Hubba the Dane 93
Hunslet Engine Company 37, 44, 68

Kenwith Castle Halt 33, 44, 62, 93, 96, 141
Kingsley, Charles 13–4, 87, 110
Kinver Light Railway 34
Kipling, Rudyard 106, 128

Light Railway & Tramway Acts 19–21, 50
Liveries 68, 71, 76
Locomotives 37, 44, 68–71, 123–6
London & South Western Railway 15–6, 18, 20, 28, 30–1, 80, 85, 123, 125
Lover's Lane Halt 56, 62, 142
Lynton & Barnstaple Railway 85

Mill, George (promoter) 20
Molesworth, Captain George Frederick (Director) 9, 18, 20, 27, 29, 33, 38, 121, 122
Mudcott (see Abbotsham Road)

Northam 38, 41, 44, 50, 55, 61–2, 110, 112, 142
Northam Burrows Hotel & Villa Company 14, 29

Pebble Ridge 14, 47, 106, 120
Permanent Way 41, 56, 87, 130
Petrol railcar, proposed use of 121

Richmond Road Halt 56, 62, 128, 137, 142
Robertson, C.L. (Director) 9, 121
Rolling stock
  Freight 44, 74–6
  Passenger 36, 43–4, 53, 69, 71–6

Sellon, Stephen (Engineer) 9, 36, 50, 122
Signalling & Signal Boxes 42–4, 52, 56–7, 77–8, 89, 91–3, 98–100, 103, 109–10, 113, 115, 130
Sowden, Henry (General Manager) 9, 55, 85, 121–2, 131
Strand Road Halt 44, 60, 62–3, 79, 130

Taylor, George (Director) 18, 20, 27, 29, 33, 38, 121
Tickets and fares 29, 78–80, 106
Train services 59, 63–8, 123

Western Counties Electric Railway, proposed 47
Westward Ho! 14–7, 20, 29, 36, 38–41, 44, 47, 54, 61–2, 67, 77, 80, 103–11, 119–20, 122, 127–8, 130–2, 137, 141
World War I 122–6

144